"If you come to a fork in the road,
take it."

Yogi Berra

## The Gift of Baja

San Diego

Mexico

United States

Baja California

Mexico

Pacific Ocean

Sea of Cortez (Gulf of California)

The Heart of Baja California, Mexico

Experience the freedom, open space, peace and adventure of the Baja California backcountry as you bike, cycle or drive the fascinating, challenging backroads.

Experience trips to the turquoise waters of remote beaches, lush ranch country, missions, Indian Rock Art sites, dramatic mountains and quaint villages.

Share the road with a vaquero heading for market with his pack animals. Give your kids the opportunity to see ranch life and how a family can live comfortably without electricity. Baby goats frolic along the road, while cheese and saddles are being made in the homes. Hike up canyon streams, kayak the dramatic Sea of Cortez with the porpoise, surf the Pacific or dive and snorkel either coast.

The 20 trips were chosen with the adventurous traveler in mind. While some of the backroads will challenge the mountain biker, motorcyclist and 4 WD driver and their equipment, others are suitable for the less experienced or those with more fragile transportation.

The Gift of Baja California, though, is available to everyone who turns even a few miles off the pavement. This person gives himself the opportunity to stand beneath a 40-foot Cardon cactus or gaze spellbound from the mountains to the sea at the magnificence of nature at its purest.

# BACKROAD BAJA

20 Backcountry Trips to
Beaches, Mountains, Missions, Ranches,
and the Indian Rock Art
of Central BAJA California

**MAPS •LOGS•TRIP INFORMATION**

**Maps and Illustrations
Bruce Brown**

**Patti and Tom Higginbotham**

For all Baja California adventurers and explorers. Those who went before and those yet to come who loved and will love and help protect this special place, always.

Front Cover Photograph by Kevin Worrall
Cover Design by David Foltz
Maps & Illustrations by Bruce Brown
Photographs: Back cover, clockwise;
Travis Cary, Tom Higginbotham,
Gustavo Nacht, Tom Higginbotham
Page 22; David Foltz

Somethin's Fishy Publications
P. O. Box 2010
Sparks NV 89432

© 1996 Patti and Tom Higginbotham
ISBN 0-9632222-3-6

*Thanks to all of our backcountry traveling buddies who made the writing of this book a pleasure with their good-natured companionship. Special thanks go to Betty and Al, Bruce and Pat, Bob and Bessie, who put up with so much when we were hurrying them or slowing them down with our log and photo stops.*

*Especially we thank Landon Crumpton . His support, computer assistance and help with production details were invaluable. We look forward to his new Baja Atlas.*

*Bruce Brown, illustrator, cartographer and good friend, gave not only his artwork but his ideas, time , patience and countless hours of proofreading.*

*Lastly, we thank the people of the backcountry who graciously invited us into their homes, gave us directions and assistance when necessary, and their courtesy and friendliness always.*

## IMPORTANT TO THE USER OF THIS BOOK

The maps and logs in this book are intended as guides and must be considered approximate. All drivers, owners and passengers of any vehicle using this book are explicitly warned that the maps, logs and trip information may unintentionally misrepresent the conditions. Everchanging road surface hazards and obstructions may not be shown or described accurately.

Users of this book drive at their own risk and use their own judgement at all times as to the safety of their backroad Baja California travel and experiences. The writers and publisher do not make any warranty, expressed or implied, as to the ultimate accuracy, safety or completeness of this information, nor take any responsibility or liability for any person or entity in connection with any actual or alleged losses or damages caused by the use of material in this book.

# Preface

"Once Baja California casts its spell, one becomes an incurable addict."

Erle Stanley Gardner
*Off The Beaten Track in Baja*

*A seagull squawks like a car alarm, already competing with his flight mate, as they pass by on their way to another day's work on the Sea of Cortez. An ambitious fellow, he rouses us from a deep Baja sleep. In the half-light of dawn we burrow deeper into the warmth of our sleeping bags, listening to the soft slap of an incoming tide. Tom, with only a little prodding, climbs out of our camper bed, switches on the portable radio and pops back in. We have only minutes before the sun will rise and erase any possible radio reception.*

*KNX news suddenly blots out the sounds of nature as the announcer transports us to the city of Los Angeles. We both know why we feel the need to hear what's going on in the fast lanes of the world: we relish the superiority of "us" over "them," the poor souls involved in the announcer's messages.*

*Time: 6:45 A.M. in Hollywood. The eastbound Santa Monica freeway is slowed to a crawl by a stalled car in the fast lane. A drive-by shooting, a double murder, the stock market's in a slump, inflation is on the rise. The mud slides of last week have been cleared from Pacific Coast Highway.... Could be the news from 1979, or 1989, the same ol', same ol'.*

*As the freeway Skywatch comes back on, we roll up our bedding and switch off the intruding voice, more interested in our local news that comes by sight, sound, smell or not at all.*

*The sun eases over the top of the craggy hills backlighting a towering Cardón cactus in its path while a lone turkey vulture perches on the tip of its tallest branch. As he spreads his wings to dry in the sun, Baja's homely garbage collector is transformed, becoming a magnificent spread-winged symbol reminiscent of the eagles atop Northwest Indian totem poles.*

*Our coffee perks, the sky awakens, changing to its favorite daytime dress of intense blue. The sand warms beneath my toes, a pelican bobs silently on the mirrored water of the Sea of Cortez and I give thanks again that of all the places that exist in the world, I found my utopia in Baja California, a mere 700 miles from the hustle-bustle lifestyle of that radio announcer.*

Utopia? Many friends have visited in our 15 years of expatriated living south of the border. Some come and go as quickly as an F-14 jet; they dart in, see no shopping malls or theater complexes and zip out again. They tell their friends back home about the boring drive. Yet most who see no beauty in Baja have never bothered to take even a tiny step off the pavement. Just one kilometer up almost any dirt road on the Baja peninsula hides miracles for the person willing to search. Maybe it's silence you find, something modern dwellers of civilization rarely experience. I often stop on backcountry hikes, waiting for even the bird song and insect hum to cease. Perhaps your miracle would be the sight of a frigate bird in mating season, perched on a high cliff, his red throat pouch blown into a red balloon to attract a mate. It could be a stand of Old Man cactus, their furry heads gathered like a disreputable rock band, or the rancher who rides up to your camp on his burro, his face bursting with the radiance of a welcoming smile.

The Baja backcountry became an obsession the first time Tom and I turned off the Transpeninsular Highway. Sometimes we travel alone, very often in the company of other backroad enthusiasts. We search the maps and atlases of the peninsula for roads we've never taken, scenes we've never seen. We repeat trips to the mountains or ranch country to visit the friends we've made. Sometimes we travel familiar roads that change with the seasons. On other trips, we challenge ourselves and our vehicles with poor roads just to see if we can make it or to discover why the road is there at all.

The more we drive the Baja backcountry the more we admire its people. We meet ranchers, many descendants of the first settlers known as the Californios, living miles from even the smallest settlement. They seem to have a comfortable and fulfilling life without the questionable benefits of our modern civilization. They raise cattle or goats, which provide them with meat, dairy products and leather. They make their own cheeses, saddles and shoes, cook on wood and light with kerosene. The men travel by mule, with pack burros, 30 or 40 miles to the nearest village for supplies.

*The backcountry teaches patience. Although Margarita, a rancher's wife, knew our next probable visit wouldn't be for more than six months, she was willing to wait for the bottle of Kerry Lotion she'd requested. A son's next baby, a fiesta at a neighboring ranch, a birthday celebration or the butchering of a goat are the events by which she measures time. She's given birth and raised 11 healthy, handsome children; they live on neighboring ranches and show the greatest respect and affection for their parents. Primitive? No. Proud, self-sufficient, content would be my adjectives.*

*Lovers of the sea will go to any length to get to a seacoast and Tom and I are no exception. Baja California provides us with two coastlines, the Pacific Ocean and the Gulf of California, or the more romantic sounding Sea of Cortez, as I prefer to call it. We have made it a game more than once to discover a route from one body of water to the other, sometimes finding it necessary to cross high mountains on roads better left to the rancher and his burros. Not long ago we decided to explore a sand dune-lined road leading to a Pacific beach. We found ourselves miles from anywhere with our 4-wheel drive wheels churning helplessly as the fine silt slowly refilled the holes like sand in an hourglass. On the positive side, we've discovered "all-to-ourself" beaches and wandered into camps of fishermen who became life-long friends.*

*Each backroad adventure is as individual as the company you keep. Alone, it may become a re-acquaintance with yourself. Sharing the tiny miracles in a tide pool or the smoothness of a sand-washed pebble can be a reaffirming of affection with the one you love. While Tom and I treasure our solo trips, we also enjoy the company of friends. They add variety, each contributing some knowledge of geology or birds or routes, songs at campfire or good-natured joking when a flat tire needs changing. Some friends are the quiet doers, others the noisy, laughing joke-tellers — but we've all been silenced by a view from the crest of a mountain road, a stand of Cirio trees in bloom, a striated sky at moonrise as dramatic as any northern lights could possibly be. The brash gold of a sunrise on the desert, with coffee on and friends gathered to share another Baja morning, brings us all together in a way impossible at any other time or place.*

*Since Baja in Spanish translates "lower", someone in the government decided it was a derogatory word: it is now considered politically incorrect to refer to the Baja California peninsula simply as Baja. We will try to change our ways whenever possible. But I wish to tell the politician, whoever he or she is, that admirers of the peninsula love those four letters that make up the magical word, Baja. It rolls pleasantly across our tongues and flows with the blood through our veins. Those four letters speak of raw, uncrowded nature, friendly pioneering people, a freedom to explore mountains, valleys, sand and sea. In all the secret crevasses of heart and brain, where politicians aren't allowed to look, our utopia will always be called*

# *Baja!*

# Contents

# Introduction

*"Other things being roughly equal, that man lives most keenly who lives in closest harmony with nature ...."*

James A Michener
*Return to Paradise*

*Backroad Baja* began with our own backroad experiences, years before the first word touched the page. Tom and I finally gave it birth when we realized how many people were dropping by with backroad questions or to ask for reprints of off-highway stories we'd written in other publications. Also, we realized how many people had the desire to experience the hidden Baja beyond the blacktop but were timid to try the dirt roads without some guidance. So we began.

We soon scratched the idea of trying to log and write about every dirt road from the border to Cabo San Lucas; first, we'd never live long enough to take on the thousands of secondary roads crisscrossing the peninsula, furthermore, many really aren't worth exploring. Boring roads do exist, lacking interesting vegetation, population, scenic beauty or destination.

This book describes and logs 20 trips of varying length and degree of difficulty, some for the busy, others for the relaxed with more time. We also limited ourselves to mid-Baja for several reasons. We've lived in the Mulege area for more than 15 years, so we've done more exploring of that region. In our opinion, the proximity of "two" coasts,

the mountain ranges, plus the sparse population and an abundance of open land is what most backroad explorers seek.

Some trips can be driven in a day or threaded together with others to form an adventure of longer duration. Most of the excursions have a destination: a mission, spectacular bay, mountain summits or a surfing beach. Many roads are a challenge: over miles of rough river bed, boulder-strewn trails, loose shale and sharp-edged rock, between volcanic slides or winding, narrow, canyon walls. We've also included other easier, yet interesting, trips that can be made in a car or even a small motorhome.

Because road conditions can change dramatically, we want to stress that our evaluations should be used as guides. Even a hard, 15-minute rain and the resulting run-off can severely disrupt backroad travel. A hurricane (*chubasco*) may change the course of a riverbed. You must always use your own judgment when you take your vehicle off the highway. We've traveled roads that friends said were a breeze, only to find them washed out, re-routed and definitely Class 3. When the government grades a new road to more efficiently move produce or seafood to market, for example, the old road very often falls into disrepair, changing its classification in a matter of months. The locals are the best source of information on a road's condition and you should believe them. When a rancher says, "*Muy malo,*" he means it is BAD!

The completion of the Transpeninsular Highway in 1973 did not destroy the explorer feeling of Baja as so many of the old-timers feared. Instead, the pavement now traveling the length of the peninsula has made it possible for the Baja California explorer to reach many jumping-off points to the backcountry in a matter of hours rather than days. Today we can explore remote areas on a one-week vacation that, previously, would have been inaccessible without a month of free time.

Thousands of miles of dirt, gravel, rock and sand roads through the outback both challenge and inform. Traveled solo, in the camaraderie of a group, or as an adventurous sharing with the family, the backroads thread their way into our lives helping to stitch us into more self-reliant, patient, tranquil beings. To really have fun, enjoy it all — the planning, the drive, the dust and that glorious dunk in the sea after conquering the trail.

Backroad explorers should prepare, however. Although many of the graded back roads can be traveled safely in a car (we know an adventurous fellow who challenges them in a Mercedes sedan), the more adapted your vehicle is to backroad travel, the better your experience. The Mercedes will not, and should not try to, go where we take our 4 x 4 Chevy truck, and we do not take our truck-camper combination over extremely soft sand roads like our friend in his specially built sand rail. Plan your outings according to your interests and your vehicle.

Hopefully, *Backroad Baja*, plus the maps and guides we've found valuable, will help with what your time and vehicle will allow. Decide if you want to see the old missions, deserted mining areas, the ranches of the *Californio* settlers, deserted seashores, guided trips to ancient Indian art, or canyons and mountains running with fresh water streams.

Recently, the Mexican government has poured money into both improvement and creation of more graded gravel roads throughout the peninsula. Although traveling these routes gets you where you want to go quickly, they're not much fun. Surfaced with heavy, sharp rock, they're often severely washboarded. If a Mexican tells you the road has *permanentes,* and demonstrates by moving his hand up and down rapidly, be prepared to shake, rattle and roll. Baja drivers say you have to drive washboard at a speed of four or 40. Anything in-between will vibrate your backside and shock your shocks.

We have included these roads in some of our trips because the destination is worth the jarring ride. Others make it possible for a sturdy, high clearance vehicle without 4-wheel drive to make some of the trips. In contrast, though, our most pleasant adventures have been over roads that often require crawling speed, trips that take eight hours to travel 40 miles — or sometimes four or five days without ever seeing another vehicle.

Tom and I hope to give you the nuts and bolts information you want and need to make these trips, along with trip logs you can follow to orient yourself so you don't get lost and are never heard from again. We've also included a reading list of Baja California and 4 x 4 information.

More important to us, we want to excite you. Backroads aren't only for Al and Bobcat Bob, two "desert rats" who would stay in the outback forever. Backroads are tests of mettle. After an outing to Malarrimo Beach, when the road was in very poor condition and our caravan of four vehicles had many mechanical problems, my editor sent my story back with a notation, "Tone this down. It sounds like a trip from Hell." When I related his comment the eight of us howled with laughter. Or I should say nine. We had taken Danny, our friend's three and a half-year-old, along on our ten-day trip. Danny had stepped out of the truck the first morning, looked around and said, "Now THIS is the desert!" A desk-bound editor could never comprehend sharing Danny's happiness, his child's curiosity with everything new from lizards to whales, or that everyone on the trip, including our three year old traveling companion, gained enormous satisfaction from overcoming the obstacles and reaching our intended destination. The backroads of Baja California are for the whole family; they're educational, adventurous, peaceful and safe, an opportunity to fall back in time to a simpler, more relaxed environment.

Leave the pavement and join the rhythm and cycles of nature. Here, you must get in touch with the land and its terrain, using judgmental skills long dormant from city life. Reading the road, avoiding a sharp rock that could destroy the sidewall of a tire, or gauging a steep grade that requires low gear are all part of the experience.

Backroading demands a watchful eye to weather. Rain in far-off mountains can threaten a flash flood in a canyon or wash out a road ahead or behind. You learn to make camp with this in mind. A high cliff which will provide welcome shade in the warm months will rob the same campsite of late afternoon sun in the winter months when warmth is welcome. Experience places your camp behind sand dunes that break the cold Pacific blows or in the open when a breeze is welcome.

The name of our book came easily, Backroad merging easily with Baja. What is more important, BACKroad does not mean OFF-road. In fifteen years our backroad travel has changed as we've become more aware of the fragile desert environment. We make every effort to keep our wheels on established tracks. We make camp in areas already used by other passersby or in an area of sparse vegetation. We dig a pit for our campfires and cover and level it when we leave. Garbage is burned or carried out. Waste is disposed of in shallow catholes. We also ask permission to camp on ranch land and make certain we close and restrain the gates we pass through.

Two organizations have given us sound environmental protection information. We try to follow their guidelines. *Leave No Trace* and *Tread Lightly!* adhere to the same principles although *Leave No Trace* stresses non-motorized activities while *Tread Lightly!* was begun by U.S. Forest Service personnel to encourage proper use of public lands by motorized vehicles. Baja California's state and federal governments have also become concerned for the peninsula's ecological well-being. To continue to use the land freely, all visitors must practice viable land use habits. With this thought in mind, certainly, we all will tread lightly and leave no trace.

# Road Classification

*The roads are classified by condition and type of vehicle recommended, as follows:*

*Class 1. Graded gravel* — *Suitable for low clearance vehicles, mountain bikes and motorcycles although there may be some jarring. This road is maintained and periodically regraded. Regularly traveled, usually going to a town, village, fish camp or numerous ranches.*

*Class 2. Graded dirt* — *Heavy-duty, high-clearance vehicle, sturdy mountain bike and dual-purpose motorcycle recommended. Low-traffic road, usually to a few ranches or a fish camp. Graded infrequently or not at all. Surface depends on last grading. This road is more apt to have potholes, loose stones or larger rocks, washboarding, broken pavement, some washouts, more steep climbs.*

*Class 3. Unimproved dirt* — *Heavy-duty, high clearance 4-wheel drive vehicle, dirt bike recommended. Occasional usage, with no grading. This road has poor and constantly changing conditions, such as drifted sand, loose shale or large rocks, washouts, heavy washboarding, detours, deep rutting and potholes. Portions may be narrow, have low overhanging branches, steep grades and switchbacks.*

# CHAPTER 1

## NUTS & BOLTS — AND SANTA LLANTA

" . . . you should really try to survive. Perishing of hunger, thirst, cold, heat, snakebite or blood poisoning out in the great nowhere has to rank as one of the least desirable ways of winding up an otherwise fine off-road trip."

Spencer Murray
*Off-Roader's Handbook*

When traveling the back roads you need bits and pieces: a jar of nuts and bolts, scraps of wire, extra oil, fluids, belts, and whatever else you can cram into your repair kit. Certainly never leave the pavement without a sizable roll of duct tape. We know from experience that it will temporarily stop a leak in a radiator hose or keep the dust from leaking through a camper window onto your bed.

Something else may be equally important, however. We've learned never to pass any of the little shrines you see by the roadside without saying a little prayer to the patron saint of backroaders, Santa Llanta (pronounced SAHN-TA YAHN-TA, ), it rhymes, and translates, "Saint of Tires"). We established this discipline after buying a set of used tires for our Chevy.

Although Tom had bragged about "their serious tread pattern" at the time of purchase, on a trip to the Pacific these marvelous looking radials were all beauty and no beast. They began erupting one after another. The questionable used tires we were forced to buy, out of desperation failed also. We made the final leg without a spare in silent prayer to Santa Llanta, who interceded and got us home. The remaining tires were given away immediately.

*Don't skimp on the equipment you take off-highway. Santa Llanta may not be listening!*

"In Time of peace in the modern world, if one is thoughtful and careful, it is rather more difficult to be killled or maimed in the outland places of the globe than it is in the streets of our great cities."

John Steinbeck
*The Log from the Sea of Cortez*

### Is It Safe?

We may as well start where my mother always does, with Bandidos! Much as I tease her, we can all get caught up in our imaginations, especially when we get off the pavement which we somehow relate to civilization and safety.

In 1978, Tom and I were stranded in mid-Baja by rain. The highway had washed out to the north and we had a four-day wait in Santa Rosalia to cross the Sea of Cortez to Guaymas on the mainland by ferry. We decided to visit San Ignacio and see some new scenery. We stopped in a little restaurant in San Ignacio for lunch, and in the course of the conversation with our waiter we inquired where we might buy some fresh lobster. He suggested we visit a fishing village on the Pacific coast where his boss was at the moment working his lobster traps. He gave us directions and told us to ask for Arturo — everyone in the village would know him. We took off across a 65 mile, tooth-jarring, washboard road and arrived at our destination with no idea where to find Arturo or where we would camp for the night. The first person we encountered as we drove into the outskirts of the small village was a boy about ten years old. When asked, he smiled and said he was the son of Arturo. He ordered us to wait and sped away on his bicycle. By now the sun was dropping toward the horizon and I was becoming a bit edgy. Ignacio, the boy, returned on a bike badly in need of help so while we waited for Arturo, Tom got out his wrenches and repaired the bicycle. The small owner thanked him and rode off.

Other than a private plane sitting on a dirt airstrip beside us, we were alone. With my vivid imagination, I even had Tom eyeing the deserted aircraft with suspicion (by now I would have mistrusted a toy poodle with ribbons in his ears). From out of nowhere a blue taxicab pulled up beside us. It held four men, each sipping from a can of Tecate beer. The driver inquired in broken English if we wanted to see Arturo, then directed us to follow him to "the house of the Americanos."

We were now more than edgy, in a village miles from civilization as we knew it, being herded God-knows-where by four sinister-looking men.

Questions jumped between us, some voiced some silent as we left the village, what there was of it. What was a taxi doing in such a remote place? Who were these men? Did this "house of the Americanos" belong to the drug-dealer-owner of the plane?

The taxi took off, and so did we. Like the girl in a suspense movie who creeps down a dark stairway knowing full well a murderer lurks below, we were committed to solve the mystery, and meet this mysterious Arturo. As we sped over a sand road on and on through a total wilderness of dark dunes we discussed the possibility of turning around and hightailing it back the way we'd come, but curiosity kept us on the trail behind the taxi.

My heart really began to pound when I finally spotted a small house sitting alone on an isolated stretch of beach. "Perfect location for a murder," I murmured. Five or six pickups were scattered about, but there was no sign of people. Tom decided to park our truck heading out the way we had come and left me with the disconcerting order, "You stay here with the doors locked. I'll go inside and see what we've gotten into." I glanced at the keys in the ignition and scooted into the driver's seat, ready for a quick getaway if he came running. But what should I do if he didn't come running, or didn't come at all? My brain was producing an award-winning thriller. The seconds seemed endless. Then minute piled upon minute. Still he didn't reappear. The setting sun, then the twilight continued to fade. My suffering increased when another pickup pulled up, and three young women hopped out in the company of two more men. These were ladies of the night, I decided immediately. Where was Tom?

Finally he appeared with the taxi- driver. With a beer in his hand! They stopped to talk to the latest arrivals. Then they were coming toward our truck, with me locked inside. "It's okay," "Tom shouted through the closed window. I was unconvinced, even though I reluctantly exited the truck and followed him into the house. The young women, introduced as Patricia, Maria and Norma didn't look like the prostitutes I'd seen walking the streets of Hollywood. We rounded the corner where I was introduced to Arturo, a man with a wide grin, who was busy cooking dozens of lobsters on a monstrous grill. Three American men from Fresno told Tom that they owned the house. They weren't particularly friendly, probably considering us party crashers, but Arturo acted like he'd known us forever and insisted we stay for the fiesta.

Although we were uncomfortable, we stayed. One by one the other men came up to talk and as the evening wore on our Spanish improved. Tom began a conversation with the sullen bearded man I remembered in the back seat of the taxi. He told us he was the doctor of the town. The doctor? Two of the other men were lobster fishermen. Vicente was an abalone diver. One of the men who had driven up with

the "Ladies of the Night," was a policeman — and the ladies were in reality the local school teachers. Chano, the taxi driver, was Arturo's cousin from Santa Rosalia who had driven over especially for the fiesta.

My mystery thriller faded, killed off by guitar music, a feast of fish, lobster and clams and friendly people.

Chano became a good friend who visits our home every time he comes to Mulege.

Vicente and the fishermen Mario and Manuel and their families are all dear friends today. We stop to see Arturo and his son in San Ignacio every time we pass by. We've stayed in touch and watched their children grow up and begin lives of their own. They've all come to visit us in Mulege.

## Is it safe?

We were camped with a group in a river bottom. Tom and Trent built a fire ring from the nearest boulders and we all gathered around a cheery blaze to tell some tall tales, a sport we all enjoy on these outings. In fact, the campfire is the perfect ending to busy days, a time to wind down before snuggling into the sleeping bag. Gail has a very funny joke that she tells with a southern accent and although we've heard it many times, we always ask to hear it again. She hadn't reached the punch line when the best imitation of gunfire I've heard rattled from the campfire. We all jumped back as the pieces of shrapnel from the rocks began shooting out in all directions. One burned a hole in the sole of Trent's shoe. We pulled all of the rocks away from the fire and one of us remembered that the water trapped in the river rocks eons ago, will boil inside and turn beautiful stones into missiles.

## Is it safe?

We were seated around another campfire eating our dinner. Tom and I were sharing a small table. I was wearing a sweatshirt with *a design on the front that glittered in the firelight. As I cut a piece of meat I felt a sudden burn on my finger. Eeyow! A spark from the fire got me, I told everyone. I shook my hand and watched a scorpion fly off onto the sand. The sting lasted a few hours, coming and going in waves. The next day my hand was slightly numb until noon, then the symptoms were gone. We decided he was attracted by my glittering shirt. Although a scorpion sting is unpleasant, it ranks far below the sting of a yellow jacket.*

### *Is it safe?*

*The chance of having something serious happen on the back-roads of Baja California ranks well below the danger of visiting an ATM machine, walking through your local park at night, or running a marathon in the Los Angeles smog.*

*Children are adored in all of Mexico. In the Baja backcountry they can run free, with no fear of molestation, kidnapping or any of those other horrible occurrences that assault our children in the states every day. They will experience a freedom many of us lost back in the '50s.*

### *Is it safe?*
### *My grandchildren and I think so.*

## FIRST THINGS FIRST
### Getting Legal and Paying Your Way

All visitors traveling south of Maneadero, which is just south of Ensenada, must have a Tourist Permit. The permits are free and can be obtained from a Mexican consulate, the Mexican Government Tourist Offices, some tourist agencies and insurance agents who spe-

cialize in Mexican insurance. You will also need a valid passport or notarized birth certificate. Minor children traveling without both parents must also have a notarized letter from the absent parent granting permission for the child to travel in Mexico. If the parent is deceased a death certificate may be necessary. I've met several divorced parents who almost had their vacations canceled for this reason so be sure to get the necessary papers.

Mexican liability insurance on your vehicle is a must. If you are towing a boat or trailer it must carry the same coverage or your vehicle insurance is invalid. You also need the vehicle registration or a notarized permit from the lien holder to take the vehicle into Mexico. Another warning: Drug or alcohol use can invalidate your Mexican insurance.

Membership in one of the travel clubs listed on page 22 will ease the preparation for traveling to Mexico. They can provide insurance, fishing licenses, boat permits, plus up-to-date information on road condition and weather, in addition to considerable discounts on hotels, restaurants and sports activities. The monthly newsletter alone is worth the reasonable yearly membership fee. Discover Baja is located in San Diego. Vagabundos del Mar operates out of the quaint town of Rio Vista in northern California. Both clubs offer RV tours to Baja California attractions.

If you are crossing the border during regular business hours, it's fairly simple to get legal fast. Stop at one of the insurance offices located along the border on the U. S. side. Buy your Mexican insurance and ask for a blank Tourist Permit. Ask the agent for directions to the nearest money exchange and change some of your money into pesos, preferably small-denomination bills. It's much easier to keep track of what you are being charged for gas when using pesos, as opposed to having to figure the exchange rate, or letting the attendant figure it for you. Exchange enough to get started, then as you're driving down the highway, stop in any town with a bank and change more as you need it. The banks give the best rate but most only exchange dollars between 8:30 A.M. and 12:30 P.M.

Immediately after crossing the border, stop at the *Migración* Office, fill out your blank Tourist Permit form and have it validated. It must be validated to be legal. The immigration officer will give you up to 180 days on the permit depending on your destination and his mood.

Many visitors to Baja California have a very blase´ attitude toward Tourist Permits and, it's true, they're rarely checked. If you should become involved in an auto accident, however, you will fare better if your paperwork is in order. You also will be asked for your Tourist Permit or passport when cashing traveler's checks.

## Where Should We Go?

We're all built differently, both physically and emotionally, and nowhere is it more evident than off the highway. Excitement to me may be ho-hum to you. Some folks love the beaches and will do anything to get there while their traveling companions don't like sand in their shoes. Before going anywhere you should sit down and make plans. Ask some questions of yourself and whoever else is going along.

I've met a few people who set tremendous goals for themselves and their allotted time. One young man decided to follow the mission trail. He was taking a year to do it. In contrast, I just read about an organized off-road tour that planned to leave from San Diego and drive the equivalent of four or more of our trips in six days. We and our friends have spent as long as 10 days on just one trip. We stopped to explore while those on the six day tour obviously are going to get their fun out of driving, and driving, and . . . .

As you must guess, we feel sorry for the people who come to Baja to escape a fast-paced frantic life-style and then carry on at the same speed as before. The back roads aren't about speed. They're to explore. If you try them at high speed, you'll miss the Baja feeling, and chances are you'll tear up your equipment and ruffle the feathers of your passenger. Too much speed over rough terrain tires the wife and blows the tires. It's wiser to preserve the vehicle you're relying on to get you in and out of the backcountry.

Our backroad trips can be taken one small bite at a time. The novice can get his feet dusty with a one day trip, or even less, close to his Baja home base. We have some acquaintances who took one of our trip logs on their first backroad outing. They came back elated with their adventure, telling us about giant Cardón cactus, a man riding a burro, the canyon where they camped out. The more they talked the more we realized they had only ventured a few miles into the ranch country behind Mulege, to places we go quite often to buy oranges or a goat. It didn't matter. They had a wonderful time and saw more of Baja than 90% of the tourists driving down the Transpeninsular Highway.

For compatibility when traveling with friends, and we've taken many trips with four or five rigs and eight to ten people, it's best to have a couple of planning meetings.

First, we establish our goal. If we're going to Malarrimo Beach, for example, we pull out our maps and all the written material we can find to decide how many days we want to spend. We discuss what we'll need in the way of clothing and camping gear. We each take responsibility for bringing certain gear and each of us makes a list so we don't arrive at our first night's camp with four folding tables and no stove.

At our final meeting we assign the people responsible for supplying the ice, water and gas and if we're sharing meals we make lists of the foods each needs to provide. Lately, we've tried a new approach to meals as an alternative to pot-luck. Each night one couple is responsible for dinner for the group. They set up, cook, serve and clean-up. All four women on our last outing preferred this system since each of us had three nights off from cooking, and only one on. We also had more variety as we all tried to make our meal special, not just more hot dogs and beans.

## WHAT DO WE NEED?
### Choice of Vehicle

In Baja you don't have to go far to get into an argument concerning the necessity of 4-wheel drive. I've sat through so many campfire "discussions" on the subject I usually retire to my bunk with a good book instead of listening or participating. Yes, a competent driver with a sturdy, high-clearance pickup can make it over many of the gouged-out, sandy, boulder-strewn backroads of Baja California, very often at the expense of his rig and tires, however, or at the inconvenience of his traveling companions who help with the digging and towing-out. We've *traveled* willingly with

friends who did not have a 4 x 4 at their disposal and we've *helped* them willingly. But when the guy sits and brags later that he can do anything with his truck that a 4-wheel drive vehicle can do, believe me he's lying -- so use good judgment.

Many of the backroad trips in this book can be traveled with two-wheel drive vehicles. Most will be more comfortable in a 4 x 4 and a few will *require* it. Trip 17, for example, is included as a test of skill and will. Do not try it without a 4-wheel drive vehicle. Do not ask a 2-wheel drive Toyota pickup, a fine highway vehicle, to climb uphill over uneven slabs of rock and boulder where slipping can be not only uncomfortable but dangerous. This type of terrain is an impossible Catch 22 situation. Without the low gearing and front and rear traction, you'd need to substitute excessive speed. The secret is to traverse upgrades over loose or uneven terrain at a creep. Four-wheel drive provides a combination of low speed and high traction.

Yes, we've heard the popular *gringo* saying, "When you break down in Baja, wait for a Mexican in a '48 Chevy to come along and pull you out." It's true the Mexicans living in the backcountry are very helpful and most do drive 2-wheel drive vehicles. It is also true that they will warn you against traveling certain roads without "*doble*," as they call 4-wheel drive. You may get help on the well-traveled stretches of backroad but we have been on many roads where we never saw another vehicle for days at a time. So don't count on being rescued if you choose to test yourself and your vehicle beyond local recommendations, unless you like to hike miles to the nearest ranch where it is doubtful the rancher will have a vehicle suitable for rescue. A 4 x 4 traveling companion is a wise decision. Pick a backroad trip appropriate to your vehicle and enjoy.

# BACKROAD CHECKLIST
* Recommended for trips of extreme difficulty

## *TRUCK BASICS*

FIRE EXTINGUISHER
WATER CAN
GAS CAN
HYDRAULIC JACK, minimum 5-ton capacity, 12-ton is much better
TOW STRAP OR CHAIN
TOOL KIT, complete with appropriate wrenches, standard or metric
TUBE OR RADIAL TIRE PATCHING KIT
LIQUID TIRE SEALANT
12 VOLT TIRE INFLATOR
TIRE GAUGE
LUG WRENCH, 4-WAY
*TWO SPARE TIRES, mounted on wheels
 ENGINE OIL

POWER STEERING FLUID
AUTOMATIC TRANSMISSION FLUID, if applicable
BRAKE FLUID
HIGH-PRESSURE HOSE FOR POWER STEERING
RADIATOR SEALANT (Have used BAR'S LEAKS™ with success).
SPARE HOSES AND BELTS (It's wise to replace all, then carry the used ones
        as spares).
*WHEEL BEARING GREASE
WD-40™ LUBRICANT, or equivalent
SPARE POINTS, CONDENSER, SPARK PLUGS, ROTOR
ELECTRONIC IGNITION MODULE
*WATER PUMP
*FUEL PUMP
MATERIAL TO REPAIR A LEAK IN THE FUEL TANK
FUEL FILTER
OIL FILTER
AIR FILTER
FUSES
LARGE CRESCENT WRENCHES
DIAGONAL CUTTING PLIERS
HACKSAW WITH EXTRA BLADES
DUCT TAPE
ELECTRICAL TAPE
CHANNEL LOCK PLIERS
BATTERY JUMPER CABLES
AUTOMOTIVE WIRE
BAILING WIRE
SIPHON HOSE
SHOVEL
HEAVY HAMMER
PLYWOOD FOR UNDER JACKS IN SAND (1' BY 1' BY 3/4")
J.B. WELD™
PERMATEX™ SILICONE GASKET MAKER

HOSE CLAMPS
A CAN OF BOLTS, NUTS WASHERS, SCREWS, TUBING, AND ANY-
    THING ELSE THAT MAY HELP A TEMPORARY REPAIR.
REPAIR MANUAL
EXTRA SET OF KEYS
FIRST AID KIT
**MISCELLANEOUS**
COMPASS

WORK GLOVES
FLASHLIGHT AND EXTRA BATTERIES
HATCHET
CANTEEN
WATERPROOF MATCHES
KNIFE
HAND CLEANER
BINOCULARS
MAPS
LITTER BAGS
SPARE SUNGLASSES
PAPER TOWELS
TOILET PAPER
CAMERAS & FILM
FIELD GUIDES
CAMPING GEAR

**PERSONAL ITEMS**
TOOTHBRUSH
TOOTHPASTE
HAIRBRUSH & COMB
DEODORANT
RAZOR
SUNSCREEN (#15, minimum)
INSECT REPELLENT

LIP BALM
SKIN MOISTURIZER
SUNGLASSES AND PRESCRIPTION GLASSES, WITH
SPARES, IF POSSIBLE
ANY MEDICATIONS YOU TAKE REGULARLY
PRE-MOISTENED TOWELETTES
TISSUES
NOTE PAD AND PENCILS
SLEEPING BAG
SNAKE BITE KIT  (Sawyer Extractor™Pump)
SPACE BLANKET
NON-PERISHABLE FOOD
CANNED DRINKING WATER
INFLATABLE SPLINT

## TRAVEL CLUBS

DISCOVER BAJA
3064 Clairemont Dr.
San Diego CA 92117.
(619) 275-4225  (800) 727-BAJA.

VAGABUNDOS DEL MAR
33 N. 2nd St.
Rio Vista CA 94571.
(800) 474-BAJA.

## Our Responsibility To The Backcountry

Two organizations deserve recognition for their efforts to inform and educate by establishing guidelines which will allow enjoyment of the outdoors while protecting the environment through minimum impact use.

**LEAVE NO TRACE** has been established to promote the educational program of outdoor skills, ethics and stewardship. LNT, Inc. is aligned with four federal agencies — the National Park Service, U. S. Forest Service, U. S. Fish and Wildlife Service, and Bureau of Land Management — who share a commitment to maintaining and preserving America's public lands.

LEAVE NO TRACE minimum impact guidelines are available on a pocket-sized plastic tag to carry with you. They also publish several helpful booklets: *Desert and Coastal Mexico* is of special interest to Baja California visitors. For more information or to order materials, call 1-800-332-4100.

### TREAD LIGHTLY! ™
### ON PUBLIC AND PRIVATE LAND

**TREAD LIGHTLY!** is a not-for-profit organization dedicated to protect public and private lands through education. Emphasis is placed on responsible use of off-highway vehicles, other forms of backcountry travel, and on low-impact principles applicable to all recreation activities. For more information, call 1-800-966-9900.

*Like these two fine organizations, we hope to encourage the minimum-impact approach to protecting Baja California's fragile desert environment. Our trips are backroad, NOT off-road. We travel established Baja backroads. We travel by 4 x 4, not to blaze new trails but to leave as little impact on the old trails as possible. We hope you will also.*

21

## The Safety Net

File a travel plan with someone before you leave on a backcountry trip. Give them the general area where you will be traveling, your expected date of return and a description of the vehicle or vehicles and their license numbers.

If you should have a breakdown or health problem, seek the nearest ranch. Some of the ranches have radio communication with nearby villages or towns and can send word via the airways.

Government medical clinics are available in all but the smallest communities. Doctors and a staff are on 24-hour call. If they can't treat the problem they will arrange transportation to an area hospital.

Air evacuation, although expensive, is available from almost any area with a dirt airstrip. The hospital staff will make a call to the air evacuation company in the U.S. After confirmation of payment guarantee, usually by credit card, a plane staffed with a doctor or critical-care nurse will arrive to fly the patient to the nearest U.S. hospital.

Two air evacuation numbers:
MASA — (800) 643-9023 or (817) 430-4655.
(Yearly insurance available).
AIR EVAC — (800) 010-0986 or (619) 292-5557.

# SECTION 1
## Ghost Towns, Beaches, Missions

*"All the other and very varied attempts to 'develop' the area ... have ended in dismal failure, for the land has always returned to its own wild self."*
Joseph Krutch
*The Forgotten Peninsula*

*We had parked to make camp in a narrow arroyo alongside a rugged, rock-faced mesa. It wasn't by accident we'd chosen a site dominated by a forest of mature and towering Cardón and Cirio. The majestic Cardóns humble one with their height and bulk while whimsical Cirios draw attention with an unusual habit of sending their branches out in every direction: some up, some down, some twisted like runaway strands of rope. In February the carrot-shaped Cirios wear a coat of thick green leaves the full length of their trunks, plus a crown of small flowers. As the sun sets below the neighboring cliff, throwing our campsite into shade, it still shined on the tip of the nearest Cirio, setting its blooms afire like the flame of a giant candle. Perhaps more than its shape caused the Spanish to name this curious plant* cirio, *after the tapered candles used in their churches.*

The ghosts towns of El Arco and Pozo Alemán add human interest to the routes for anyone interested in snooping around old mining towns left much as they were when the lucrative minerals gave out. In Pozo Alemán, small caves dug out of the cliffs by mine workers still house bunks softened by layers of paper and old clothing. A blue enamel coffee pot sat over a makeshift cook top as if its owner had just departed. The locked buildings house an undisturbed collection of mining equipment. Sometimes the area is populated by a caretaker, or several families. Other times, as on our last visit, no one was about.

The beaches of the Sea of Cortez from San Francisquito to Bahía de Los Angeles lie mostly undisturbed save for the flotsam from the sea. Local *pangas* at Bahía de Los Angeles are for hire to visit the numerous off-shore islands. The bird rookeries should be approached quietly and only from a distance to avoid disturbing the mating and nesting seasons.

Remote Misión San Francisco de Borja combines the old Jesuit chapel and hospital founded in 1759 and the newer Dominican addition

El Arco Church

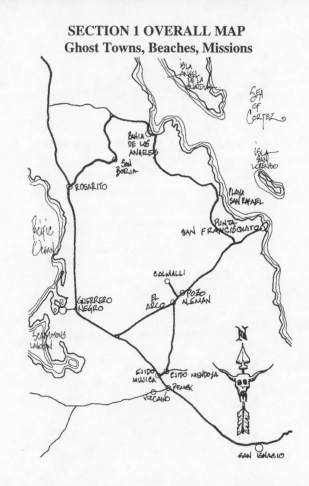

added in 1801. Completed rejuvenation stands side-by-side with areas of eroded adobe and crumbling mortar. Donations from the occasional visitor help with restoration costs. The amount of reconstruction and maintenance in such a remote area is quite remarkable. Masses are still held in the chapel by a priest who rotates through the area once every several months.

Little changed, this section of the peninsula provides a sample of the Baja California traveled by explorers long before the paving of the Transpeninsular Highway.

# TRIP 1
## The Mountain Mining Towns
(from Highway 1 at Ejido Francisco J. Mujica to
El Arco, Calmallí and Pozo Alemán)

" ... the long rugged Baja peninsula ... may be pictured as a symbol of the failures of human endeavor that plagued the peninsula . . . for nearly three hundred years."

Howard Hale
*Long Walk to Mulege*

*Although the goal of this trip is a visit to the mining towns, the desert scenery and lush vegetation invite hiking. To thoroughly enjoy the backcountry we feel compelled to take to our feet. Only then can you marvel at the tiny pink and lavender blossoms of Sand Verbena since they bloom at toe-tickling height. On foot your eyes have time to assimilate nature's landscape architecture. The rock tipped by eruption eons ago protrudes from the ground like the riffled pages of a book. The thrill of finding a stand of Pitahaya when the prickly fruit is ripe, then slicing one open to sample the sweet, crimson pulp takes us back to the days when the Indians gathered to gorge for days on this watermelon-flavored, once-a-year treat. Nowhere do the spirits of these ancients, now extinct, killed off by drought, starvation and the white man's diseases, seem closer than when we travel the trails they must have walked upon through the beautiful but demanding desert.*

The gold-seekers ascended these hills in the early 1900s, tearing up the landscape with their mines, building El Arco into a town for the 1,000 or so new residents of the area. Calmallí turned up the richest strike. The gold and copper was hauled across the Vizcaino Desert to the port of Santo Domingo, north of what is now Guerrero Negro.

When the rich strikes dwindled all but a few miners departed, leaving the area scarred but peaceful again. Elephant trees, Cardón, thick Cholla and a multitude of desert plants remain, however, along with the clear days and quiet, star-studded nights. To enjoy the mining town visits even more, the book, *Long Walk to Mulege*, written by Howard Hale after his adventurous journey down the peninsula in 1921, introduces us to some of the residents of that period.

**Trip Length:** 32.4 miles to Calmallí.

**Road Condition:** Mostly Class 2 with sporadic Class 3 sections of rough, loose rock. Rutted with high centers in parts, often due to past flooding. Difficult in wet weather.

**Supplies & Facilities:**
  **Fuel:** El Arco sporadic. Fuel at Vizcaino turn-off.
    Note: If continuing on to San Francisquito and Bay of L.A., be sure you are carrying sufficient food, fuel and water.
  **Supplies:** None.
  **Lodging:** None.

## Trip Log

*Highway 1, Km 154.5 at Ejido Francisco J. Mujica, to El Arco, Pozo Alemán, Calmallí*

0.0     Km 154.5, 6.6 miles north of Vizcaino on Highway 1, turn north onto dirt road across from Francisco J. Mujica. Signed: "Guillermo Prieta 23". The road begins Class 1, flat, straight, graded gravel. Sand roads parallel it in many places and are often preferable to heavy washboarding if the grader has not passed by recently. Ball moss engulfing many of the Yucca and Cardón indicate the presence of dampness and fog at times as it rolls in from the Pacific.

7.5     Turn left just past the small group of block homes, Ejido Angel Aramburo Mendosa. You will see an old water pump on the corner. The road quickly turns to Class 2 which could be a problem during rainy weather as evidence of prior flooding indicates. It continues straight as a cactus spine toward the mountains, through a Yucca- and Cardón-dotted desert. *Garambullo,* known as the "Old Man" because of his showy head of white, abundant Cholla, and the tall, segmented Candelilla add interest along the route.

21.8    Short stone wall on the right hints at civilization.

22.3    The structures of El Arco can be seen in the distance. The road is a little more rocky and rough. The mineralization of the area becomes more apparent with the beginning of quartz fragments strewn along both sides of the road. In spring the Brittlebush brightens the landscape with its vivid yellow daisy-like blooms.

22.8    A stone marker on left is followed by a dirt airstrip.

24.4    The scattered town of El Arco and its cemetery come into view, along with the skeletons of mining equipment and trucks.

24.9    The small church in El Arco shows present-day care and tending. Flowers beds are in bloom and a mining wagon containing copper rests within a circle of carefully chosen and placed quartz rocks. Mining areas into the sides of the hills are evident in the surrounding area and sporadic mining for gold and copper is reported to still take place. A small road crew is *sometimes* in residence in the town. They can *sometimes* supply emergency fuel from barrels but it is best not to count on it. Although a small population is reported, more often than not, this once flourishing gold mining center is deserted. It's difficult to believe that at one time over a thousand miners were working in the area. Class 2 road to Pozo Alemán.

26.9    A very important fork in the road at Pozo Alemán area. Note the windmill landmark. Left goes to the buildings of Pozo Alemán (German town) and the ghost town of Calmallí. Right continues on to San Francisquito. Where Trip 2 begins.

# TRIP 1 MAP  The Mountain Mining Towns

## Side trip to Calmalli

0.0  Take left fork toward Calmallí the town that produced $3 million in gold back in the 1920s. A Class 3 road, rutted tracks, high center, some wash-outs.

4.6  The remains of an old mine.

5.2  Note the silhouettes of old cars at final rest on the hills. We identified an old "Woody", a Model A Ford and Chevys from the '40s. CAUTION: A beautifully built, VERY DEEP well remains on this site.

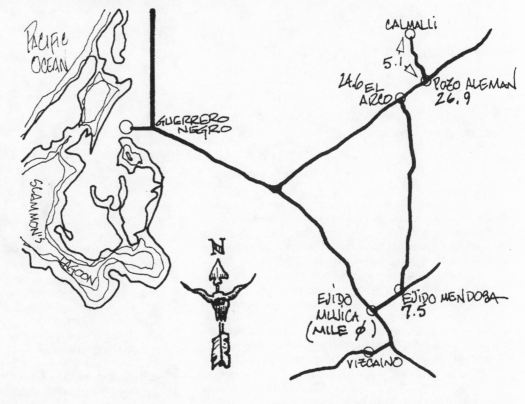

PACIFIC OCEAN

SCAMMON'S LAGOON

GUERRERO NEGRO

CALMALLI

5.1

24.6 EL ARCO

POZO ALEMAN 26.9

N

EJIDO MUJICA (MILE Ø)

EJIDO MENDOBA 7.5

VIZCAINO

# TRIP 2
## Pozo Alemán to Bahía San Francisquito

"From where I stood there was no visible evidence that the earth was inhabited."

Joseph Wood Krutch
*The Forgotten Peninsula*

For scenery, the trip to San Francisquito would log in on the World Wide Web with something like http://www.scenery/dramatic/. Volcanic mountains provide vibrant vistas of deep valleys thick with green Cardónals (forests of Cardón cacti). The giants numbering in the thousands spread as far as the eye can see.

Cardón reaching 50 feet are said to be 200 years old. Built with a rib structure that can expand to take on water and contract to conserve the supply, this relative of Arizona's giant Saguaro is an efficient desert survivor. Once the plant dies, the hardwood ribs dry into the desert dwellers' wood supply. Ranchers use the long straight sticks for fences, the walls of their houses and corrals. They build tables, chairs and beds of Cardón and burn it in their wood stoves. This imposing cactus blooms with a white flower in the spring, a fuzzy fruit appears in summer.

The dipping, twisting branches of the Cirio make it the most unusual plant on the peninsula. Also called the "Boojum Tree" after a character in Lewis Caroll's "The Hunting of the Snark," the Cirio shows its most dramatic whimsy along this road. Cirio by the hundreds soar to the heavens, branch into grotesque fingers, return to earth in arches fit for a wedding ceremony. If this plant could be described as lovely, it would be after a rain when it quickly dresses from tip to toe in a coat of bright green leaves which it sheds quickly to conserve moisture. The flowers in late spring and summer range from white to yellow They often appear red, however, with a setting sun and could be mistaken for a flame at the top of the tapered candle.

*We camped just east of Pozo Alemán with our friends, Al and Betty, in a quartz field. Over thousands of years the deposits have washed down the hills with each rain adding more to the snowstorm on the desert. Walking through this treasure trove of dazzling deposits is like shelling a new beach. At first I picked up every delightful chunk. Then I became more selective. Although I had my eyes riveted to the ground most of the time, the extensive desert hikes revealed many discoveries. I startled jackrabbits, cottontails and quail, and Harris Hawks on the hunt themselves. I identified the paw print of a mountain lion. An hour later, three deer leaped down a steep cliff into my path. Another day a desert grave surrounded by a crude picket fence, it's wooden marker faded beyond reading, inspired a sadness and curiosity about the person. Did he spend his life in this remote location or was he a passerby like me?*

*Al coached us and we begin to search for 6-sided crystals. I shall never forget my first find. There it lay, its perfect facets glistening in the sun. It was small and a bit chipped from its tumble down the arroyo, and a little yellowed from who knows what. But it was such a discovery, no diamond could have seemed more lovely!*

**Trip Length:** 46.7 miles.

**Road Condition:** Mostly Class 2. Okay for high-clearance 2-wheel drive vehicles. Lots of washboarding, some steep grades and washes.

**Supplies and Facilities:**

**Fuel:** San Francisquito, at the harbor in barrels, sometimes but don't count on it. See Alberto Lucero.

**Supplies:** No stores. Possible meal at " Las Cabañas de Puerto San Francisquito". Maybe a cold beer or soda. Very often, not.
**Lodging:** Small cabañas on the beach at "Las Cabañas". Camping and/or showers.

# TRIP LOG

*Pozo Alemán to Bahía San Francisquito*

0.0   Begin at the fork at Pozo Alemán (signed,) left to Calmallí, right to San Francisquito. Take right fork.

0.3   Cemetery. Here you will see many of the old Baja California surnames, the Aguilars and Villavicencios who settled the peninsula. Many graves are quite old with no markers, others are marked with fine quality granite headstones. One man passed away in 1974 at the age of 98. The road continues as a combination of Classes 1, 2 and 3 — up, down and irregular.

2.0   Widespread area of mineralization. Quartz scatters every where. Road continues flat and straight with some washboarding.

5.0   Flat sand road through area of very tall, mature Cardón and Cirio forests. Some of both species reach heights of 30 to 40 or more feet. In addition, this Baja California garden produces luxuriant sections of Palo Verde, Ocotillo, Ball Moss, Barrel and "Old Man" Cactus. On one Cardón we estimated to be 50 feet tall, we counted 33 branches.

16.0   Rock garden of giant boulders, Cataviña before the graffiti painters.

17.0   Stone corral on left. Worth a stop to walk inside and see the innovative construction using some of the giant rock formations as a portion of the walls.

19.5   *SIDETRIP: TO WATERHOLE, STONE CORRAL AND DRAMATIC STEP-DAMS.*   Turn right. 4.4 miles in and out.

20.5   Ranch on right. Fire has destroyed the yucca forest on both sides of the road for miles.

26.3   Road curves through rocks and boulders in a National Park-quality setting.

26.6   Steep grade.

26.8   Gate and small chapel on right. A good place to touch bases with *Santa Llanta*. From this vista the road drops into a valley with a straight sand road. You can actually "speed" along at 25 mph.

29.6   Fork on left. Connects to graded road to Bahía de Los Angeles. Badly washed out. Continue straight on badly washboarded sand. This is another "4 or 40" mph road.

34.7   Rancho El Progreso, a yellow ranch house with windmill. Bear left.

35.4   Bear right onto graded road. This is another government road that depends on the frequency of the grader for its quality. A sand road parallels it in places and is often smoother.

46.7   San Francisquito. Turn left at Private Property sign to harbor. To go to the beach and Las Cabañas, turn right and drive on left side of airstrip, then go left on sand road to the waterfront.

Sea of Cortez

San Francisquito
(46.7)

35.A

29.6

34.7
RANCHO
EL
PROGRESO

26.8

20.5    RANCH

19.5

19.0

N

EL ARCO

STONE
CORRAL

POZO
ALEMAN
( MILE Ø )

31

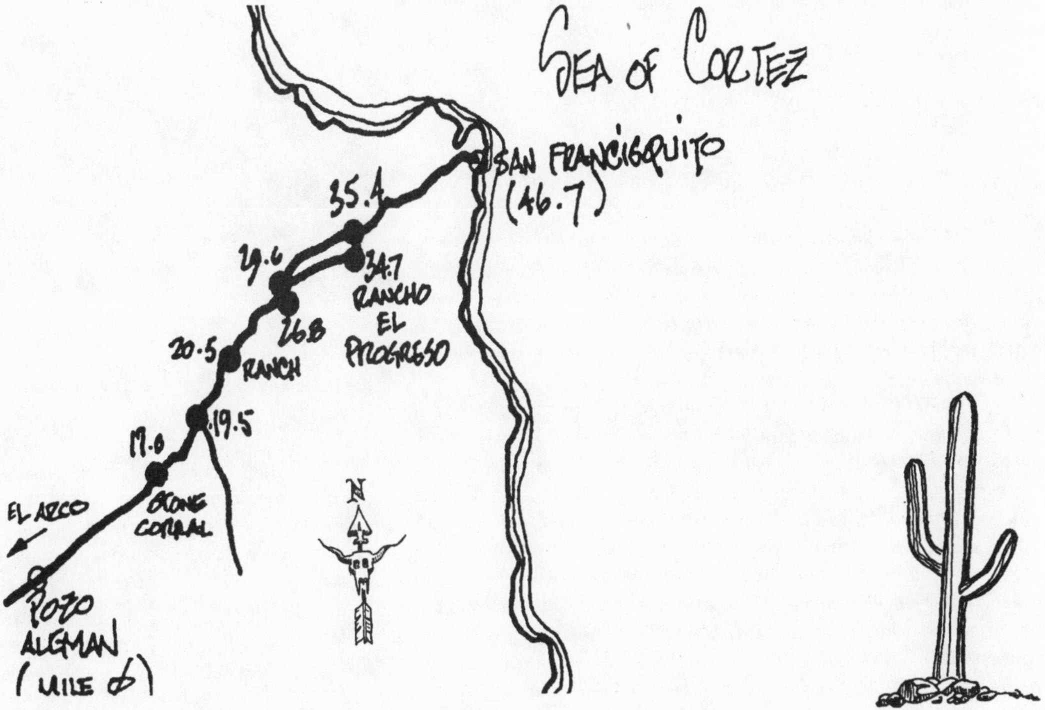

# TRIP 3
## Bahía San Francisquito to Bahía de Los Angeles

*"There's always manana and no one here is worrying about today!"*

Ray Cannon
*The Sea of Cortez*

*We had camped at Bahía San Rafael the night before in a wash leading to the beach. In the night we were reintroduced to the area's famous winds. They come with force, this time bringing a hard rain along. In the morning we faced an exit through sticky sand and mud. No 4-WD, no get-out! The government graded road looked mighty good when we reached it and were on our way again.*

*Bahía de Los Angeles is an outpost, a destination promising citified luxuries to outback travelers. After seven days of backcountry we drove into the village, found a campground that promised a hot shower, cleaned up and headed for the nearest watering hole. The six of us ordered cold beers and Margaritas, sipping the icy liquid with relish, then trooped around town, visiting The Diaz compound where Mama and Papa Diaz began the tourist business many years ago with a small hotel and restaurant. They catered to fly-in fishermen and the stout-hearted who drove the rough old road before paving spread down the peninsula. A few other establishments eventually sprang up but Bahía de Los Angeles is still a laid-back, out-of-the way resort that* caters mostly to fishermen. The Pemex station promises gasoline but sometimes runs out. Pangas are available for fishing or excursions to the numerous and fascinating off-shore islands, if the guide is in the mood. Like many of the backcountry villages, life moves slowly.

A field studies program conducted by Glendale Community College brings students to Bahía de Los Angeles each year to study marine biology, natural history and the history and geography of the area. The student input has been a great help to Bay of L. A.'s museum. Constructed with contributions from the locals and visitors, *Museo de Naturaleza y Cultura* houses an interesting collection of old photographs and leather work including tanning vats and saddles. The collection includes mining equipment, ore samples, wearing apparel, shells, geological samples, arrowheads and whale bones, plus Cochimí Indian artifacts and history. The sale of books and T-shirts helps with maintenance expenses.  The museum, manned by volunteers is open afternoons. Carolina Shepard Espinoza, a long time resident, is often in the museum and a very informative curator.

**Trip Length**: 83.4 miles.

**Road Condition**: Mostly Class 2, slow speed. Some Class 3 areas with washouts, very rough. Several steep grades and drifting sand. This coastal area is often subject to strong north winds which could hamper the mountain biker's or motorcyclist's progress. Because of sparse traffic the road is not well-maintained.

**Supplies and Facilities:**

    **Fuel:**    San Francisquito in barrels *sometimes*.
              Bahía de Los Angeles, Pemex station.
    **Supplies:** Markets and restaurants in Bahía de Los Angeles.
    **Lodging:** Motels and campgrounds in Bahía de Los Angeles with hot showers.

## Trip Log
### *Bahía San Francisquito to Bahía de Los Angeles*

0.0    From sign "Private Property", follow road back toward El Arco.

13.1    Turn-off on left to El Barrill.

13.3    Road left to Rancho El Progreso and back to El Arco. At this junction, continue on road bearing right.

20.7    Vistas of the approaching mountains begin. The road is not washboard but has some washouts and switchbacks. Very pleasant at slow speed. Sections are difficult with slippage in 2-wheel drive. Some areas are prone to heavy drifts of sand.

37.7    Road on right leads to a fish camp on the beach.

40.4    Road on right turns down to sand beach on Bahía San Rafael. Midriff islands in view. Possible campsite behind the dunes or on the beach with a 4 x 4 or bikes. With any threat of rain this is not a good choice without 4-wheel drive, and even with it sticky mud and sand could cause a halt.

41.0    Road begins to climb a steep grade.

43.4    View of wide alluvial plain, the beaches and off-shore islands. *Isla Tiburon* off the mainland coast stands out plainly. Low gear recommended for steep downgrade and use caution as there are some areas of caved-in road surface on the drop-off side.

43.9    Washed out arroyo with crude repair. The length of road between San Francisquito and L. A. Bay is in disrepair with a narrow road bed due to the large half-moon-shaped

*33*

washouts along the edge. The scenery and lack of traffic make up for the detours.

48.4　Arroyo shows signs of major flooding. Boulders and mature trees litter the dry wash. The road continues through a wide valley toward the mountain peaks in the distance.

55.0　Km 45 marker. Washouts demand slow speed. Two-wheel drive is risky, especially if traveling alone.

### SIDE TRIP 3.7 miles in and out

60.9　*A green car door on the left is a sign for a road to the left that runs along the foot of the mountains.*
*Turn left, then turn right at the first canyon road. 4 x 4 recommended. We call this "The Canyon of Balancing Mudballs." You'll see for yourself, these giant marvels, three dams, plus well-constructed stone corrals. Take a hike! Return to the "main" road and continue on.*

60.9　Km 35 The well-graded road continues through *Valle Las Flores*, the valley of the flowers, with *Sierra La Libertad* on the left, *Sierra Las Animales* on the right.

72.7　Las Flores. Silver mining in this area in the late 1800's produced millions. What remains today is a smelter and boiler and the stone vault used to store the silver. No thieves could make it through the building's 3-foot thick walls. On our last trip, from El Arco to this point, we didn't pass another vehicle in either direction.

83.4　Pemex station. Bahía de Los Angeles.

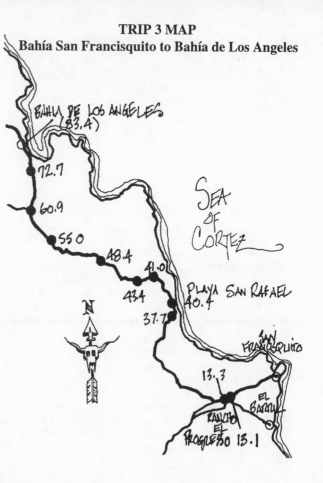

## TRIP 3 MAP
## Bahía San Francisquito to Bahía de Los Angeles

# TRIP 4
## Bahía de Los Angeles, Misión de San Borja

" . . . so much to explore, to see, to study in Baja California . . . may you participate in this history by helping to preserve it intact: its old Missions, its pictographs, its picturesque scenery, its exotic plant life . . . . "

Tomas Robertson
*Baja California and its Missions*

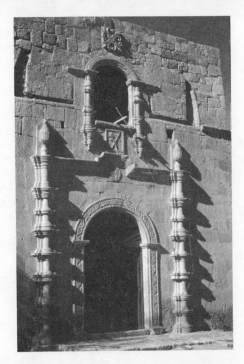

We travel the narrow road through a choke of thick brush, *Cardón* and *Cirio*, to this isolated setting chosen by the Padres. After entering the hushed buildings, a kitten causes a start as it scampers through leaves on the stone floor. Was it really the cat or could it be the long-gone Indians and Padres that cause an involuntary shiver on a warm day? Perhaps meeting with the adobe and stone puts one in touch with the spirit of their creators.

On this roughest of roads on a sunny day in February after a hard rain, the occupants of the three trucks in our caravan stopped to make a sandwich and grab a cold drink. Bessie stepped out of the truck onto a perfect quartz arrowhead. The sun shining through the peeling bark of the elephant trees has turned it to golden parchment. After stopping to make camp, in no hurry to leave this enchanted land, we hiked through the Cirio forests, marveling at their grotesque shapes.

Our usual campfire bonding seemed the strongest of any evening of the trip. Undoubtedly we felt the presence of those who had come before: Indians, the Padres, the Spanish, who made Baja California their home.

## Misión de San Borja

Misión San Francisco de Borja Adac was born, survived and grew under the direction of three different orders of Spanish Padres. This Mission was funded by the bequeath of a wealthy Spanish Duchess, Señora María Borja, upon her death in 1747. At the sight of a spring of water the Indians called *Adác*, Father Jorge Retz of the Misión de Santa Gertrudis opened a road and built a church, storeroom and small hospital. From the start it was very difficult to support the converted Indians who came there to live, although the Padres raised corn and cattle and received some help from Misión de Santa Gertrudis to the east. In addition they planted orchards of figs, dates and olives. By 1764 the Mission area was responsible for over 1,000 Christian Indians.

The expulsion of the Jesuits turned control of the Mission over to the Franciscans in 1768. Then on June 12, 1773 Misión de San Borja was handed over to the Dominicans who added the newer masonry church.

Today periodic rebuilding continues, helped along by the donations of passersby. Much has been stolen including the church bells.

**Trip Length**: 43 miles.
**Road condition:** Some Class 2, mostly Class 3. Very difficult for bicyclers. 4 WD recommended.    Steep grades of loose, sharp rock. Uneven road surface, washes, deep ruts and holes. Very slow speed required. Recommend traveling in company with another 4 x 4.
**Supplies & Facilities**:
    **Fuel:** L.A. Bay.
    **Supplies:** L.A. Bay and Rosarito.
    **Lodging:** L.A. Bay.

### Trip Log
*(from L. A. Bay to  Misión San Borja to Hwy 1 at Rosarito, Km 51.)*

NOTE: Leave Bahía de Los Angeles on road leading north. At junction, bear left on paved road leading to San Borja turn-off and Transpeninsular Highway 1. San Borja turnoff, 14.1 miles from L. A. Bay.

0.0    Turn left on road to San Borja Misión (signed). This road begins as Class 2, narrow with loose rock.

2.0    Road on left. Continue straight.

2.1    Class 3. Very rough grade. 4 x 4 necessary to make the climb. Dramatic Elephant tree forest followed by field of Jumping Cholla with vista of wide valley.

3.5    Deserted ranch (at time of writing).

4.0    Highly mineralized area. Good dirt road with some waves rather than washboard and a few deep holes to slow progress. The road continues through a dramatic Elephant tree forest.

10.1    Class 3. Road rough with sharp rocks that can bruise sidewalls. Ascend through loose schist,  2 WD not recommended.

10.7    Continuous potholes. Deep and muddy after a rain. Road narrow and overgrown with cacti and brush. Necessary to keep windows closed to prevent injury from passing branches.

| | |
|---|---|
| 14.7 | A road to right.  Bear LEFT. |
| 15.3 | Tricky little upgrade made worse by loose rock.  Much of this portion is 2 mph speed.  After a rain, the deep potholes become watering holes for cattle. |
| 17.9 | Loose schist downgrade. |
| 19.5 | Very irregular road surface through arroyo.  Care and slow speed necessary.  Ball moss appears on the Boojum trees along with a cool breeze from the Pacific.  Bad climbs and descents continue with short sand reprieves in-between. |
| 21.9 | Misión San Borja, a majestic reward for tough driving.  To continue on to Rosarito and Highway 1, take either fork west from the Misión; both meet at Rancho San Ignacito. |
| 27.6 | Rancho San Ignacito  (Signed: "Elevation 380 S.N.M. , Km 10 Mil 6)".  Smooth sand road passes beneath arbor of over-hanging mesquite trees. Vehicles with campers use care. |
| 28.5 | Cross wash of river rock and sand. |
| 30.0 | Sign facing toward Rosarito (Misión San Borja Km 17). |
| 31.6 | White water tank on right.  Road is deeply rutted sand and river rock. |
| 39.9 | Road smooths out, thankfully. |
| 40.8 | Road bears right at corral. |
| 43.0 | Transpeninsular Highway 1 at Rosarito, Km 51. |

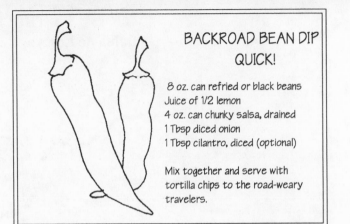

## BACKROAD BEAN DIP QUICK!

8 oz. can refried or black beans
Juice of 1/2 lemon
4 oz. can chunky salsa, drained
1 Tbsp diced onion
1 Tbsp cilantro, diced (optional)

Mix together and serve with tortilla chips to the road-weary travelers.

# TRIP 4  MAP
## Bahía de Los Angeles to Misión San Borja

MEX. HWY 1

JUNCTION TO BAHIA DE LOS ANGELES

JUNCTION TO MISSION SAN BORJA

SEA of CORTEZ

BAHIA DE LOS ANGELES

2.1

3.5 (RANCH)

14.7

30.0

27.6

31.6

21.9
MISSION
SAN BORJA

40.8

ROSARITO

43.0

RANCHO SAN IGNACITO

PACIFIC OCEAN

N

# SECTION 2
## The Vizcáino Desert, Scavenger's Beach and the Pacific

*"Baja gave me an intermittent, fleeting glance into another world...of spiritual experience a thousand times more different from my old rational, logical, scientific conception of reality."*

Graham Mackintosh
*Into A Desert Place*

Strange how different life is in sparsely populated areas. We don't hesitate to ask a rancher we've never previously met if our friend can park the trailer for his sandrail next to this man's house while we make the trip to Malarrimo Beach and back. He is delighted to be of help and invites us in to meet his sons, Paco, Gabby and Alonzo; yet in our own country we can't park our camper in a brother or daughter's driveway for even one night. Neighborhood restrictions consider it, and us too, probably, an eyesore.

Last year we again met Paco on the road near his father's ranch. We stopped and chatted briefly before turning off for another Malarrimo adventure.

Our friend, Ray, had Jeep troubles from the start. First a flat tire, then NO brakes. Although the line had developed a leak he managed to keep going with care and the use of his low gear. The road was very rough in spots and at one point we noticed one of the milk crates he had tied on the roof rack had tipped over. Ray checked it but decided he hadn't lost anything important so we continued on, reaching the beach in time to do a little exploring. It was a cold day and even after we set up camp well back in a canyon, the wind swirled through our site whipping a tarp/windbreak and rattling our tents and campers. Dark clouds traveled in front of the sun, a barrier to the little warmth available. We hurried to heat our meal and make a campfire.

*After dark, as we sat as close to the fire as possible, we thought we could hear a vehicle approaching. In such a remote area, someone traveling that road at night was unusual and a little disconcerting to all of us. The motor noise grew louder and then out of the night a 4 x 4 Toyota, customized with 3-tone paint and graphics pulled up to our campsite. Three young Mexican men got out of the truck and walked toward us. In the dark we didn't recognize Paco or his two friends. The biggest surprise, though, was the six gallon container, 4 cans of oil and a flat fixer cartridge that they carried. Ray took one look and said, "THAT'S what fell out of the milk crate on top of my Jeep." The young men explained that they had found the items on the road and Paco realized they must belong to us. They were afraid we would need them so they drove 26 rugged miles in the dark to bring them to us. Although we offered them food and drink, they declined. They went on to the beach to camp for the night and stopped by in the morning on their way back to their homes.*

## Now that's the Baja Spirit!

The people of the Pacific are pioneers. Some have dug wells and built homes, carving out a modest ranch life for themselves. Others have migrated from the inland towns of San Ignacio and Santa Rosalía, for example, to join the life of the small fishing villages along the Pacific where lobster and abalone offer a hard but lucrative livelihood. Each of the villages have formed cooperatives to control the catch and size limits of the area. The fishermen must belong to the co-op and abide by their regulations. This has had a positive effect on the conservation of the seafood, most of which is shipped to the markets of the Far East.

### MARIA'S LOBSTER BREAKFAST

2 Tbsp margarine
4 slices bacon, chopped
1 onion, diced
4 cloves garlic, minced
1 tomato, chopped
2 California chilis, chopped
1/2 tsp oregano
1/4 tsp black pepper
2 cups lobster, cooked and chopped
2 cups potatoes, cooked and chopped

*In a large skillet, fry bacon until limp but not brown. Add onion and garlic and cook until onion is transparent. Add tomato, chilis, oregano and pepper; stir and cook about 2 minutes. Add lobster and potatoes; heat through, stirring to mix. For breakfast, serve with scrambled eggs and hot tortillas. For dinner, serve with hot tortillas and tossed salad. 4 servings.*

*Our visits with fishermen friends and their families in these villages often becomes a cooperative effort. We bring the beer, produce, staples and meat — items the locals enjoy which are expensive for them to buy. In turn, they contribute lobster or abalone in season — items we enjoy which are expensive, or impossible, for us to buy. Their ladies make tortillas and ours make fresh salads, since fresh produce arrives only sporadically to their pueblos.*

On our last visit to a small settlement along the coast, we entertained the entire village at our camp, all seven families! Now, is that something to tell your grandkids?

Although the vegetation of this area of the vast Vizcaino desert would best be described as sparse, one has only to look a bit more carefully at the beige landscape. After a rain the undulating sandy plains turn a brilliant magenta with the bloom of Sand Verbena, bordered by the brilliant yellow of Brittlebush daisies. The ground-hugging verbena creates a brilliant patchwork contrast to its dull surroundings. Often, just when the sand becomes monotonous, as on the road to Malarrimo Beach, you suddenly pass a pebble-paved mesa overlooking a deep canyon of rusts and golds; or you say "definitely arid country", then come upon a stand of Elephant trees in bloom. I must mention these grand pachyderms now since in every set of my Malarrimo notes they come up. I write, "...twisting through a canyon of low hills populated with mature Elephants, their bark glistening silver in the sun..." The Pachycormus discolor, one of the three genera found on the Baja peninsula, is the largest of the elephant trees, so-called because

of their thick, short trunks, and stubby twisting branches which are reminiscent of an elephant's trunk. Their fleshy stems enable them to collect and retain water; like most desert plants, they combat evaporation by bearing leaves only briefly. In spring the Pachycormus discolor blooms a brief but brilliant pink, which is quite spectacular when seen in mass with other trees. Although the Elephant tree further protects itself by producing a strong-smelling sap which repels grazing animals, when hiking I find the aroma from a brush with an Elephant refreshing and have thought of gathering some for a Baja potpourri.

Jatrophae, or Lomboy, the smallest of the genera, is a shrub with no resemblance to the tree. Lomboy have long, wispy branches which are usually bare except after a rain when they rapidly produce and then shed a large showy green leaf. The sap of the Lomboy is used by the locals as a medication to treat chapped lips and skin rashes. When Graham Mackintosh, the fair-skinned redheaded Englishman who walked 3000 miles around the Baja California coast, met the heat of the peninsula, he suffered terribly with swollen, sunburned lips until he met a rancher who introduced him to the wonders of the Lomboy sap. He began applying the sap to his lips daily before hiking and had no more trouble. Tom, another fair-skinned redhead of English descent, has suffered with fever-blisters of the lip consistently during our sun-exposed Baja years — until Graham introduced him to Lomboy. Now he can go out in the noonday sun without suffering the cracked, bleeding lips he had decided was his Baja burden.

   The winds of these areas cannot be ignored. While they annoy, they're also the artists, creating mouth-parching landscapes of striated dunes, whipping up frothy salt ponds, swirling the countryside with an occasional "Dust Devil", a magnificent, dry tornado spinning upward in a spiral of sand. We stop to watch a raven dive into a canyon then pop up on a thermal and glide. Then we continue, feeling the soft trauma when our wheels again meet sand drifted across the road.

   Untamed, uncrowded, and bursting with the Baja spirit, this area begs return visits.

## Mad Dogs and Englishmen Go Out in the Baja Sun Armed with the Sap of the Lomboy!

# SECTION 2  OVER ALL MAP

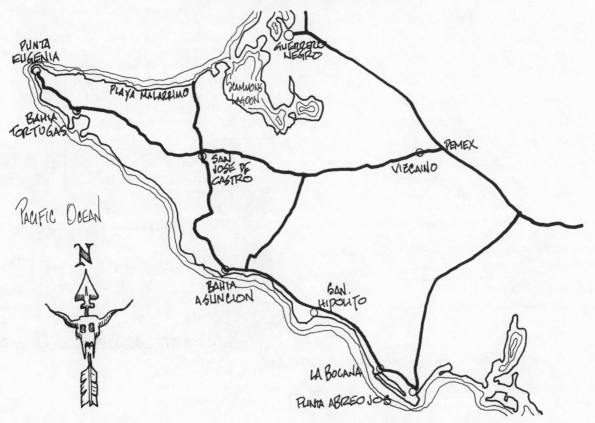

PUNTA EUGENIA

PLAYA MALARRIMO

BAHIA TORTUGAS

GUERRERO NEGRO

SCAMMONS LAGOON

SAN JOSE DE CASTRO

PEMEX

VICCAINO

Pacific Ocean

N

BAHIA ASUNCION

SAN HIPOLITO

LA BOCANA

PUNTA ABREOJOS

43

# TRIP 5

## Vizcaíno to Bahía Tortugas and Punta Eugenia
(from Km 144 on the Transpeninsular Highway 1 to Punta Eugenia)

### "Cana al aire!"
Javier Zuniga

Whenever we tell our friend Javier at the Las Casitas Hotel in Mulege that we're off on another backroad trip he always says, "Ah, cana al aire!" This Mexican expression translates literally, "We're going to throw a grey hair into the air." Since all of my friends tend towards Clairol, I think its meaning is more like "Ladies Night Out" or "We're out for fun." So whenever we take off across the Vizcaíno road, I try to ignore the washboard and dust and think positive thoughts about what's to come. Cana al aire!

Although this area of the Vizcaíno desert has little color and sparse vegetation, sand dunes rippled by the wind and the quiet, uncrowded, unspoiled landscape have their own appeal — especially to city dwellers. We often walk out on blinding salt flats where a photo of us wearing ice skates and a muffler would really fool the folks back home.

I grew up in Ohio where a mirage was a wave of heat over a country road. My first trip across these roads where lakes and islands appear and disappear right before your eyes is a Midwesterner's wonder of the world. Tom and I always make wagers on what is real and what is not as we close in on Scammon's Lagoon and 90% of the time we're both wrong.

Since the plants of this region must protect themselves against heat and minimal moisture they can't often afford the luxury of leaves and flowers which allow evaporation. After a rain, though, like aging movie stars, they light up the scene with their short-lived but showy display of colors. In the late afternoon, when shadows accent the undulating mesas and hills spreading one after another toward the horizon like the ripple of velvet, an appreciation for this type of desert cannot be denied.

Bahía Tortugas is one of the friendliest towns on the Baja Peninsula. Even the houses seem to be of good cheer, painted a variety of pastels, with smiling faces in every doorway. The bay is a stopping-off anchorage for privately-owned cruising boats traveling north and south on the Pacific so it's rare not to meet a "yachtie" or two in the town. The beaches are wide open for camping but a 4-wheel drive vehicle is recommended if you plan to pull out onto the sand on the trails the locals have been driving. Many Mexicans along the Pacific coast have 4 x 4's they drive onto the beach for clamming or tending nets so don't be misled into thinking these sand trails are solid. You can get stuck fast, especially in the section of soft, dry sand that always precedes the wet, hard stuff nearer the water.

Once you reach the coast, the Pacific view takes over and you care little about the lack of vegetation although the dry, stark, rolling knolls along the coast also have a beauty of their own. From the small village of Punta Eugenia you can continue a few miles to beautiful camping on bluffs above a photogenic rocky shoreline. The small

off-shore island of Natividad is home to a surfing camp and a yearly surfing contest while Isla Cedros, the large island to the north, houses a cannery and large lobster fishery. The live catch is flown to Ensenada. It's possible to hire a panga to visit the islands in good weather.

We returned to Eugenia one afternoon after visiting the farthest navigable point by vehicle. We'd stood on the top of a bluff mesmerized by the Pacific waves crashing ashore below us. Then we stopped to watch an elderly man and his grandson mending a net they had stretched across one of the flat bluffs above town. Its regular openings, rather than catching fish, had become miniature picture frames outlining segments of sea and sky. We sat for many minutes just watching the peaceful work, the ocean, the comings and goings of the pelicans and gulls. If someone were to ask what's in Punta Eugenia? I'd be quick to answer, not much and yet everything.

**Trip Length**:  106.6 to Bahía Tortugas; 122.9 to Punta Eugenia.

**Road Condition:** Class 1. Suitable for mountain bikes, dual-purpose motorcycles, and motorhomes, even, if the owner doesn't mind the shaking and a few loose screws . The first 21.2 miles have been paved recently but some potholes are already present. The road then becomes graded gravel with severe washboarding in places. It is the typical "4 or 40" mph government road. Speeds in-between are killers that shake your vehicle and passenger into foul moods. This is a road that gets you where you want to go . . . Period.

**Supplies and Facilities:**
    **Fuel:** Vizcaíno, Bahía Tortugas.
    **Supplies:** Small markets and restaurants at Vizcaíno
          and Bahía Tortugas.

**Lodging:**
> **Motel**: Vizcaíno, Bahía Tortugas.
> **Campground**: Vizcaíno.

# Trip Log

*Highway 1, Km 144 at Vizcaíno to Bahía Tortugas and Punta Eugenia.*

| | |
|---|---|
| 0.0 | Km 144. Pemex station at Vizcaíno turn-off. Proceed west on paved road toward the Pacific. Yucca plants predominate on the water-conserving gray Vizcaíno desert. Don't get too used to the paving. |
| 21.2 | Paving ends; graded gravel, washboard begins. At times it is more comfortable to drive on the sand roads that parallel the gravel road. Sometimes they're better, sometimes not. |
| 34.3 | A natural salt pond on right. |
| 36.9 | The salt flat. Always be careful of oncoming traffic on these government roads. Although traffic may be sparse, the locals often drive at high speed and not always on their side of the road. |
| 39.3 | Mirages begin. |
| 46.1 | Signed road to Bahía Asunción. Continue straight toward Bahía Tortugas. |
| 51.1 | Laguna Ojo de Liebre off in distance on right.  Km 82. |
| both | Notice the Elephant tree forest scattered across the sand on sides of road. |
| 61.5 | THE Shrine to Santa Llanta I mentioned in Chapter 1. A little praying here got us back to Vizcaíno without a spare tire. |
| 64.7 | Rancho San Pedro, signed. |
| 72.0 | Malarrimo turn-off at small sign on the right. |

| | |
|---|---|
| 72.5 | San. José de Castro, signed.  Road to left goes to the ranch and on to Bahía Asunción.  Here the road smooths.  Easy enough for a passenger car. |
| 75.6 | Rancho Santa Monica, on right. |
| 77.2 | Rancho San Miguel, on left. |
| 79.3 | Puerto Nuevo, signed. Road left leads to small fishing village. The fishermen harvest fish, lobster, and abalone in season. Members of this cooperative have joined in an experimental program with a California-based company to raise abalone in a hatchery, then plant them at sea. After some failures they now have a 20% or more success rate. |
| 84.5 | Sign, "Microóndos Indios — 5 Km". A maintenance road leads to the top of the mountain and the microwave tower. This road is usually passable for outstanding views of the area. |
| 103.4 | View of Bahía Tortugas and the peninsula. |
| 105.2 | Bar Los Pinos, on left.  A reported house of ill-repute. |

*(If you want to go to the beach, proceed past the bar and turn left on a dirt road, then take right fork to Tortuga Bay beaches. The left fork is a graded road around the bay to the tip of the peninsula on the other side. The road is bowling-alley- smooth and flat skirting the bay with many areas to pull out onto the beach. At 6.6 miles from the Bar Los Pinos turn-off, at the corner with a shrine, you can go straight to Thurloe Bay, known for Pismo clams, or turn right and continue around the bay on the road between the two bays. At 9.1 miles you will reach an oyster farm! The buildings are often deserted but if you stand around long enough a panga or truck will arrive with a couple of workers who will sell you all the oysters you want to buy, cheap. It's a fun drive or ride even if you don't like oysters. )*

| | |
|---|---|
| 106.6 | Radio Tower. If you need gasoline, turn right on the second street past tower, one block to Pemex station. Otherwise, turn right to continue to Punta Eugenia at blue building, *Alimento NUTRINO*. |
| 106.8 | Bear right and continue on well-traveled road. |
| 107.3 | Fork. Bear right to Punta Eugenia. Left goes to airstrip. The road is smooth and graded. |
| 114.1 | Road on left goes to Punta Rompiente. |
| 115.7 | Beautiful vista of the Pacific. Isla Natividad to the left, Isla Cedros to north. |
| 122.9 | Village of Punta Eugenia. A picturesque town with natural harbor. Follow road to right and uphill for a view of the harbor and boats. Continue on. |
| 124.9 | Road ends at a turn-around overlooking a sand beach below with no vehicle access. |

## TRIP 5 MAP
## Vizcaíno to Bahía Tortugas and Punta Eugenia

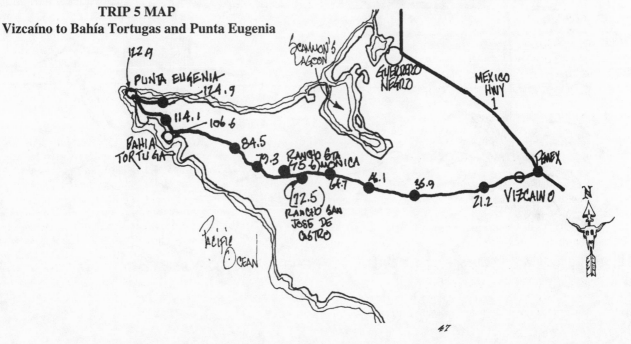

Lots of space with few people, that's Baja.

Dix Brow
*Boating in Mexico*

# TRIP 6
## Malarrimo Beach, "The Junk Yard of the Pacific"
*(From turn-off at Vizcaíno, Km 208 to Malarrimo Beach)*

**"Believe whatever you hear about junk found at Malarrimo, it's all true!"**

Spence Murray
*The Western Boatman*

We'd read stories of Malarrimo Beach for years. Of how the Japanese current carries flotsam and jetsam from as far as Alaska and drops it off on this north facing beach along Baja California's Pacific coast. The books tempted with the possibility of finding glass fishing floats and notes in bottles.

They didn't prepare us, though, for the wind that tossed us with a face full of sand and a cold blast the moment we stepped out from behind one of the continuous sand dunes that line the shoreline. We learned quickly how the sand dunes and flotsam and jetsam arrived — powerful Pacific waves, pushed by powerful Pacific winds.

We've paced off a 30 foot redwood log, certainly not indigenous to this area, and stomped around on the wooden deck of a ship. One of our group discovered a partially buried airplane, another a Cadillac Coupe de Ville. Ed found a bottle tossed off a ship as a scientific experiment of "National Geographic World" and Trent uncovered ANOTHER bottle from a California girl looking for a pen pal. So Malarrimo was all we'd imagined. We still have an unopened gas mask canister and the bright orange hatch cover from a ship; today it frames a photo of our group of Malarrimo explorers.

We've visited three times: one was an eight hour trip because of some vehicle breakdowns, plus the necessity to tow 2-wheel drive vehicles out of the soft sand; trip two took only four and a half hours since there were no drifts; the drive for this log was easy going in but with a strong wind blowing, tricky coming out because sand had drifted across the road in just a few hours. So there are times when 2-wheel drive vehicles may not be able to make it all the way to the beach. Even 4x4's are not immune to sticking; Malarrimo sand is a fine powder, "easy to get in, hard to get out." We do not recommend that 2-wheel drive vehicles travel this road alone. We also do not recommend driving vehicles, except those set up for sand, on the beach. Carcasses of abandoned trucks voice their half-buried caution. Areas of quicksand also are present. Our friend, Ray, on his Honda motorcycle, cried out for help on one of our outings and we were barely able to rescue his bike before it sank. So drive the beach at your own risk.

*49*

**Total Distance:** 26.5 to Malarrimo Beach.

**Facilities and Services:** None.

**Road condition:** The miles to Malarrimo Beach vary from season to season and year to year. The road is rough and rocky in spots but these areas can be traveled by high clearance vehicles at slow speed. Nearer the beach, the sand drifts across the road; at times it becomes impassable to all but vehicles designed for that purpose.  A beautiful mountain bike and dual-purpose motorcycle trip, but expect strong wind.

## Trip Log

Turn-off, 72 miles from the Pemex at Vizcaíno. [See Trip 5] Watch carefully for turn-off, a dirt road, on the right, marked by a small hand-painted sign. Reset trip log to zero.

| | |
|---|---|
| 0.0 | Turn right and follow sand road as it twists through a canyon of low hills decorated with Elephant trees, their bark glistening silver in the sun. |
| 2.0 | Fork. Stay left. Rocky section of road follows with dips and some high centers. |

• • • • • • • • • • • • • • • • • • • • • • • • • • • • • • • • • • • • • •

### Patti's Tip Of The Day

Tie a large bandana around your neck, cowboy-style, for this trip. When you get into the blowing sand, wear it bandit-style over your mouth and nose.

• • • • • • • • • • • • • • • • • • • • • • • • • • • • • • • • • • • • • •

| | |
|---|---|
| 3.8 | Sometimes a bad wash-out area, usually uneven moguls. |
| 4.8 | Series of washes begin with rough, loose rock. |
| 5.6 | Deep canyon on left. Here you curve into the chilly ocean breeze. The road continues with rough, loose rock. |
| 8.1 | This is THE viewpoint down into the canyon and out to the Pacific. Here you realize that your Malarrimo visit is going to be controlled by the wind. It dictates the clothes you wear, the bandana we mention, and the speed a bicycler can maintain. Chicago can't even come close to Malarrimo for being windy. |
| 11.0 | A descent with narrow switchbacks and tight corners. |
| 12.4 | This washed out area of exposed boulders should be taken at a crawl. The road continues along a sandstone mesa, oozing waves of red rock as if a giant iron gave the hills a good pressing. |
| 17.4 | Another river bottom washout, exposing more boulders to be crossed. |
| 19.2 | Areas of drifting sand begin. These vary with the wind. There are several areas where the road forks around drifts. We cannot recommend which fork to take since that varies also. It's best if in doubt to stop before the drift and walk both sections before going on. |
| 26.5 | The beach. Driving on the beach is not recommended. Those planning to camp will find it more comfortable to backtrack into the canyon far enough to get out of the strong beach wind. |

# TRIP 6 MAP  Malarrimo Beach

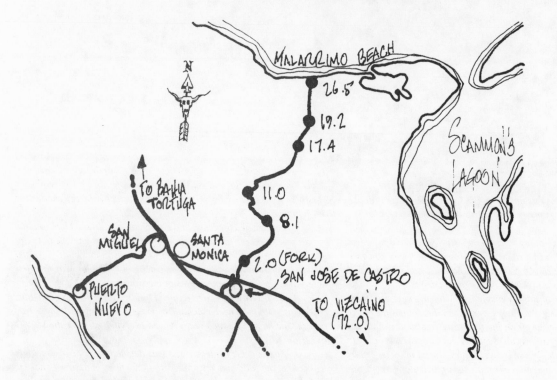

MALARRIMO BEACH

26.5

19.2

17.4

11.0

8.1

2.0 (FORK)
SAN JOSE DE CASTRO

TO VIZCAINO
(72.0)

N

TO BAHIA
TORTUGA

SAN
MIGUEL

SANTA
MONICA

PUERTO
NUEVO

SCAMMON'S
LAGOON

# TRIP 7
## San José de Castro to Punta Abreojos to Highway 1

"Being stuck is like being pregnant. You either are, or
you aren't."

James T. Crow & Spencer Murray
*Off-Roader's Handbook*

Let's call it a memorable husband/wife life experience. One of those
glaring, blame-placing memories we'd like to, but will never, forget.
STUCK!

We were zipping along on a 40 mph stretch, about four miles
out of Asunción when I looked seaward and remarked, "Why don't we
turn off on one of these roads going to the water, to see what kind of
shoreline it is? There are probably lots of good campsites."

Tom didn't seem unduly displeased with the suggestion although he did remark that the dunes were a good clue that the shore
would be windy. He turned off on the first sand road and wound out
through a maze of crisscrossing intersections, each apparently going to
another section of beach. We saw several jury-rigged markers left by
surfers or fishermen to make their return to a particular site easier.
Finally, we came closer to the dunes and, where the road became softer
stopped to turn the hubs on the 4-wheel drive. Reassured of pulling

power, we continued on. The road made an immediate turn into soft
powder. Our Chevy, heavy with camper, dove into a deep rut and sank.
Tom and I stared first at each other and then at the back wheels, resting
hub-deep in the sand.

He returned to the driver's seat and tried all of the "get-out"
tricks but the rear wheels continued to bury deeper. I could feel the guilt
of a poor suggestion riding on my shoulders as I went looking for
something to give the wheels traction while Tom got out the hydraulic
jack and began raising the rear end to make room between the wheel
and the ground for whatever I could find . We were thankful for the
square of plywood Tom always brings along to support the jack and felt
confident we would be on our way again in minutes.

I dragged several sizable pieces of sheet metal from a deserted
fishermen's campsite. We wedged the metal, some cardboard and small
rocks under all of the wheels and dug the soft sand away wherever
possible to make for easier exit. We were smiling again as we looked at
our handiwork.

Tom started the truck and eased it into reverse. I had to jump
out of the way to keep from being assaulted by the shrapnel the tires spit
out as they buried themselves deeper. Like obstinate children, they'd
tossed sheet metal, cardboard and rocks out of their way in their
determination to dig deeper holes in the sand.

We tried again -- and again. Digging deeper holes each time.
It was as if the 4-wheel mechanism wasn't working although Tom
assured me he had cleaned and greased everything before the start of
our trip.

After a terse conference, it was decided that one of us should
walk out to the road and get some help in the form of a tow. I chose to
go while Tom continued to dig. I made my own markers at each
intersection of deserted sand trail leading back to the highway to assure

I could find my husband again. At that point I wasn't sure he wanted to be found, at least by me. Let's say there were no tender good-byes between us as I departed.

Reaching the main road, I again marked the turnoff with two plastic water jugs on a long pole I stuck in the sand and began to walk in the direction of Asunción where we had one acquaintance we were sure would lend a hand.

Interestingly enough, on this isolated stretch of remote peninsula I had no fears of accepting a ride with whomever came along. My only fear was that no one would come along. It was strange to walk on a main thoroughfare with no traffic passing from either direction. I'd walked for about ten minutes, psych-

ing myself into the possibility of arriving back in Asunción by late afternoon ,when I saw dust coming toward me.

When I could see a vehicle in front of the dust I began waving and couldn't believe my eyes when a Chevy Blazer 4 x4 stopped beside me. A man and woman and their teenage son definitely looked puzzled to see an American woman alone, flagging them down. I explained the problem in my best Spanish and they immediately invited me into the back seat beside Mario, their son. We quickly reached my water jug

marker and were back to the camper before Tom had a chance to miss me.

Tom quickly pulled out our tow chain, Mario and his dad helped us scoop more sand away from the exit tracks and after minor strain on the Blazer, we were out. We insisted Alonzo, the dad, should take some money for his trouble and with many thanks the family began to leave. Luckily, Tom thought to stop them. We had one more soft spot to pass through so he asked Alonzo to wait until we were back on hard ground. Sure enough, down we went again, digging the same deep holes. Alonzo was getting a bit weary of us by now but he politely hitched up and pulled us out again.

Then we all heard a hiss and his smile dropped. One of his bald tires had run over a sharp seashell and was losing air at a rapid rate. Now Tom helped them change to their spare which was worse than the others, and gave him $25 to buy a good used tire. When Alonzo, his wife and Mario waved good-bye for the last time, we were sure they hoped not to run into anymore "gringos."

As Tom and I repacked our tools and equipment we continued to puzzle over our truck's lack of pulling ability. "The left hub just doesn't seem to lock," he kept saying. I tried it yet another time and agreed. "What's this?" I asked, "looks like a screw is coming loose."

"Nothing," Tom answered, "there was a screw missing and I didn't have the right length so I put that one in. It couldn't make any difference..." I stared him down. "Well, maybe it could," he conceded.

He found a screwdriver and removed it. The hub turned and locked and my partner looked like one of Little Bo Peep's flock, definitely sheepish.

I didn't say a word. My guilt for getting us into this situation lifted off my back and flew away into the sunshine.

We headed for Punta Abreojos and after a traumatic day were anxious to go on home. Halfway along the washboard road leading to the highway we came across two young Mexican men standing beside their pickup waving us down. Their truck had stopped and wouldn't start with the old battery they had. Did we have jump cables, water for their leaking radiator and duct tape?

After some lengthy tinkering, because of the condition of their vehicle, and after profuse thanks for the help and the cold drinks from our cooler, they were on their way again.

On the backroads of Baja, "What goes around, comes around" is certainly a truism.

**Trip Length:** 95.1 miles to Punta Abreojos: 148.8 to Transpeninsular Highway 1.

**Road Condition:** Mostly Class 1. Gentle hills and curves from turn-off at Rancho San José de Castro to Asunción. Road is fine gravel over sand with little washboarding. Some washboarding thereafter, mixed with salt flats and sand. From Punta Abreojos to Highway 1, the heavy gravel road is usually severely washboarded. Easy backcountry road for everything from mountain bikes to sturdy autos.

**Supplies and Facilities:**

> **Fuel:** Asunción, La Bocana and Punta Abreojos, sometimes.
> **Supplies**: Small stores and restaurants in all three communities. It's often necessary to scout around for the owners.
> **Lodging**: None.

## Trip Log
*Rancho San José de Castro to Asunción, Punta Abreojos and Transpeninsular Highway 1 at Km 98.*

0.0 Signed turn-off to Bahía Asunción by way of Rancho San José de Castro. This wide, 2-lane road is well-graded and maintained.

2.5 Rancho San José de Castro. The dormitory used to provide housing for local miners but the ranch is mostly deserted now. Pay no attention to a road sign with an arrow pointing to G Negro right and B. Tortugas, left. It is obviously someone's idea of a joke. No road exists and the directions are incorrect should you choose to go overland. This 40 mph road gently curves through a wide valley with hills on both sides. Blue sky, clean air and the surprising pink of Elephant trees during the blooming season.

9.6 Slow down. Road narrows to one lane through a series of curves. Don't be complacent about oncoming traffic; you will meet an occasional vehicle and some of the backcountry folks do drive fast.

11.8 A sudden view of the Pacific in the distance makes this a pleasant lunch stop. This is a fun road to drive or ride, with dips and slight curves and a fine gravel surface over sand.

| | |
|---|---|
| 22.3 | Road surface changes to decomposed granite for a short distance. Note the immediate roughness. Thankfully the sand returns quickly. |
| 23.5 | Fork. Road to right goes to San Pablo. Bear left toward Asunción. |
| 25.6 | A ranch on left with a few palms and small chapel. Here the terrain is flat and the road is wide and smooth. |
| 31.3 | Fork in the road. You can take your choice since they rejoin. We suggest you stay left although the surface is granite washboard. The right fork is sand, deep in spots and very dusty. Now the Pacific with off-shore islands comes into view. |
| 34.9 | A junk yard of abandoned military vehicles. |
| 35.4 | Aeropuerto, signed, back to the left. Km 62. |
| 36.3 | Approaching Asunción. A sign reads, *"Ceapa para cuidar el agua contamos contigo,"* which translates, "Know to take care of the water. We count on you." A message anyone who spends much time in the backcountry can appreciate. |
| 36.8 | Junction. Turn left and back at an angle, following the sign to La Bocana 70 Km to continue on to Punta Abreojos and Highway 1. Turn right to go into the town of Asunción. You will find gas on right, a market and restaurant on left. As you continue toward La Bocana there are many sand roads out to the beaches of Bahía Asunción. Use caution; the sand is very soft and powdery in spots! The main road parallels the ocean and runs straight with heavy washboarding. During the winter months, the gray whales pass close to all of this Pacific shoreline as they travel to their breeding grounds in San Ignacio and Magdalena Bays. Their waterspouts are seen easily from shore. |

| | |
|---|---|
| 40.7 | Fork. Left to Vizcaíno on graded road. Continue straight to La Bocana and Punta Abreojos. (Right about here is where we turned off to see the beach and got stuck!) |
| 43.9 | Three-pronged fork. Take center one. |
| 44.8 | Palm Oasis Rancho on left. Ocean, right. |
| 55.2 | A small point juts out into the Pacific in this area, the site of two villages, Punta Prieta and San Hipolito. At the first fork stay left to Punta Abreojos. The right fork takes you to Punta Prieta, a small fishing village, however, it will also pass through San Hipolito and return to the main road. |
| 55.4 | Fork. As before, stay left to Punta Abreojos. The right fork goes to San Hipolito, the home of Alonzo, our sand savior. |
| 59.2 | This is a second entrance to San Hipolito. Left continues to La Bocana and Punta Abreojos. |
| 62.6 | This salt flat is one of the most dramatic mirage territories you will ever see. |
| 83.7 | Cemetery. |
| 84.4 | La Bocana. Gasoline available on this corner from jugs. Turn left. Pass medical clinic and small harbor on right. |
| 86.1 | Sand drifts over road in this area at times. |
| 87.7 | Restaurant-bar on lagoon. Road is smooth as a bowling alley as it crosses extensive salt flats. Islands and lakes appear and disappear as more mirages work their magic. Caution: Stay on the traveled road. This area looks deceptively hard but it can be a hard crust with moisture underneath that will quickly bury the wheels of a vehicle. |
| 95.1 | Punta Abreojos. At first street with a stop sign you have a choice. Turn left to go directly to Highway 1. For the scenic route, continue straight ahead to the beach. Turn left or right, |

through the village. Punta Abreojos grew into a village of lobster fishermen and abalone divers. They have formed a strong cooperative and police their own against poaching and taking undersized catches. Their plant processes lobster, abalone, clams and scallops in season. The majority of the catch is trucked to Ensenada, then sold to the Far East. The Japanese and Taiwanese demand for a live catch has complicated shipping and raised the prices. Sometimes legal seafood can be purchased at the cooperative building on the beach. Continue on the salt flat/air strip, past the orange restaurant of Florinda on the left. Best lobster tacos you'll ever eat. She will appear and open up if you're hungry Pass the old baseball field on the right, their new one on the left.

96.6    Turn left on the well-traveled road that is almost at the end of the airstrip.

97.0    Bounce across the famous Abreojos washboard past the cemetery on the right. (At this point on our last trip a screw dropped out of the sun visor into Tom's lap.)

103.0   Turn-off to Campo René (La Experience Club). Campo René, in better years when the owner, René, was still living, was a unique outpost camp with its own airstrip. In addition to a row of tiny cabins of many colors, looking like Monopoly houses, Campo René had a large, screened meeting room/kitchen with wood stoves and barbecues where guests arriving by air or road could cook, eat, play cards or just visit. They could also fish for corvina or mullet off the back porch, dig scallops in the lagoon and Pismo clams from the beach. The airstrip is still usable but the rest is in disrepair. Now the Campo René area has been taken over by the Salt Works of Guerrero Negro with plans for miles of salt-drying ponds and a mile-long pier nearby for loading the salt onto ships. Controversy reigns over the effect this vast change will have on the breeding habits of the gray whales in nearby San Ignacio Lagoon.

Many secondary sand roads parallel the main road from Punta Abreojos to Highway 1. Some are smoother, some aren't. It's a guessing game as to which will be more comfortable. Be careful with speed. At high speed the washboard can suddenly throw the vehicle off into the soft berm left by the grader along the sides of the road. On one trip we saw a Ford Bronco that had rolled for this reason.

118.0   Small chapel on right.

125.8   Ejido settlement, Emiliano Zapata II, on left. Rough road here!

148.8   The time to say Hooray! Pavement! at Km 98.

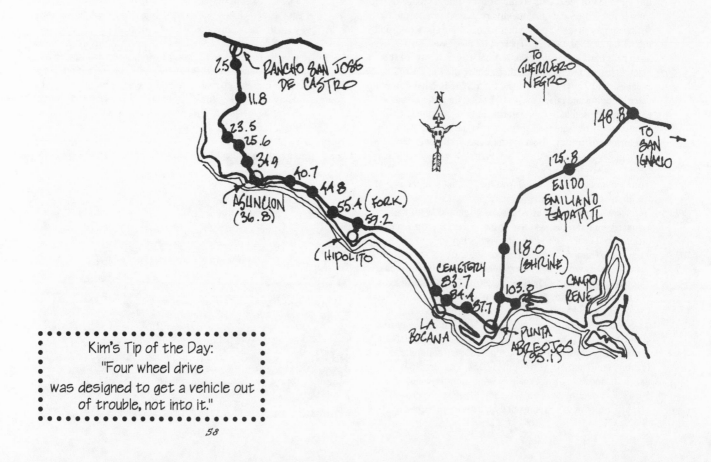

RANCHO SAN JOSÉ DE CASTRO

2.5

11.8

23.5

25.6

31.9

40.7

44.8

55.A (FORK)

59.2

ASUNCION (36.8)

(HIPOLITO)

CEMETERY 83.7

84.A

87.7

LA BOCANA

103.8

CAMPO RENE

118.0 (SHRINE)

PUNTA ABREOJOS (95.1)

EJIDO EMILIANO ZAPATA II

125.8

148.8

TO GUERRERO NEGRO

TO SAN IGNACIO

N

Kim's Tip of the Day:
"Four wheel drive
was designed to get a vehicle out
of trouble, not into it."

# A CALIFORNIA  GRAY WHALE FACTOID

- Travel 7,000 to 10,000 miles from the Arctic Sea to the lagoons of Baja California, Mexico to mate and give birth.
- Four months of feeding in the Arctic.
- Six months of commuting.
- Six weeks to two months in the south.
- Swim 4 to 5 knots in shallow, 20 to 30 fathom water.
- 40 to 50 feet in length.
- Weigh 40 tons.
- Life span 25 to 40 years.
- One of the 10 different species of baleen whales.
- Eat plankton, krill, small fish and crustaceans.
- Gestation period of 12 to 13 months.
- Calves weigh one ton and are around 15 feet in length at birth.
- Mother's milk is 55% fat for rapid weight-gain.
- Pacific gray whaling began in 1845.
- Whaling ceased in 1890's as whales were thought to be extinct.
- Gray whales discovered again in the 1930's and almost wiped out.
- Saved by International Agreement in 1938 and a ban on commercial whaling in 1946.
- In 1952, herd estimate of 2,794.
- In 1957, herd estimate of 4,417.
- A gray whale population of 18 to 20,000 at present.

We tasted tea made from the Cardón and bought a box later to treat gastritis, hepatitis and whatever else ails us.

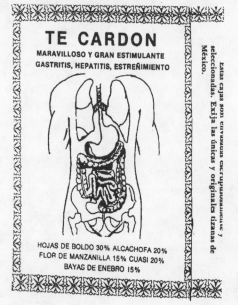

## TRIP 7A
## Mule Trips and Indian Rock Art
(Highway 1 at Km 118 north of San Ignacio to San Francisco de la Sierra. Watch for sign, "Pinturas Rupestres".)

*"I respect a mule because he looks and thinks before he steps."*

*Anonymous miner*

*Both excited and apprehensive, I gazed into the soft brown eyes of Victoria, my mule, and worried she would take an instant dislike to me. Instead, it was Richard and his white mule that were incompatible. She laid back her ears and stalked in anger until Lupe, our guide, had Richard and Dave change steeds. Then all was calm.*

*We were learning about the life of the mountains of the San Francisco de la Sierra as we traveled into the deep canyons where the ancient ones left their dramatic rock art. The ride was everything I'd expected: educational and exciting, scary and spiritual. I gave myself over to Lupe and Salvador, our guides, and Victoria, my sure-footed transportation. They watched over me carefully with a light-hearted yet serious confidence that took all of my apprehension away.*

Both men come from a heritage of mountain travel and guiding. Evenings in the canyon under the palms beside a fresh water stream, Salvador described his ranch, five hours away by mule and shared his great knowledge of the desert and mountain plants.

Salvador, fascinated with our packet of Handiwipes, then showed us the cup of water he could squeeze from the leaves of the *Siempre Viva* plant when he wanted to wash his hands. Lupe and Salvador enjoyed the food we'd packed in, especially our home-made spaghetti, but were amused by how much we needed. They travel for days with a few tortillas and some goat cheese.

The drive along the rim of Baja California's grand canyon on the way to San Francisco tempts one to arrange for a guided mule pack trip. The site of the Great Mural region of Indian rock art rediscovered by the famous mystery writer, Erle Stanley Gardner, lies in the canyon below, amongst flowing streams and giant palms. The grandest cave of all, *Cueva Pintada*, a 200-foot long grotto over-painted with stampedes of animals and human figures, showcases the mysterious heritage created 500 to 1,000 or more years ago by a now extinct tribe of peninsula wanderers.

The guides are Sierra men, descendants of the first settlers. They travel the trails into and out of the canyons on a daily basis, tending their ranches and animals. The mules are the sure-footed transportation; the burros carry the loads. Although you should be reasonably fit to make the mule trips, you don't have to be an experienced rider. The mule does the looking and thinking.

A permit to visit the paintings in the canyons, by mule, must be obtained in advance in San Ignacio. The office is adjacent to the mission church just off the main square in the museum of the *Instituto Nacional de Antropología y Historia*. For advance information on trips, the telephone/fax number is 91 (112) 2 73 89. Usually, Spanish only is spoken. The museum, completed in 1995, is open daily, 9 AM to 4 PM, except Sundays. It houses excellent photographs of the Indian rock art, plus an impressive reproduction of the rock wall and paintings of *Cueva Pintada*.

If time or physical limitations do not allow a mule trip, it is possible to visit one rock art site, *El Raton*, which is located along the road and very close to the village of San Francisco. A guide from the village will escort you to the cave and also to the homes of the leather workers on nearby ranches, if you are interested. Our friend, Richard, had a pair of desert boots made for himself while we were on our four day mule trip. The men of this region are skilled leather workers, creating riding crops, saddles, chaps and leggings.

Only twenty-three miles off the pavement lies the gateway to not only the ancient history of the primitives but a glimpse into a present day society of proud and knowledgeable settlers living well and in harmony with their environment.

**Trip Length**: 23 miles.

**Road Condition:** Begins Class 1, continues Class 2 with loose rock, high centers, steep climbs and switchbacks.
**Supplies and Facilities:**
    **Fuel**: None.
    **Supplies**: Small markets for staples.
    **Lodging**: None.

# TRIP LOG

*Highway 1 at Km 118 to San Francisco de la Sierra*

0.0 Turn off west at Km 118. Signed: "San FCO De La Sierra 37". As usual, a severely washboarded government road leaves the highway, soon paralleled by a more comfortable sand road. The washboard continues through Yucca trees, scattered Cardón cacti and thick desert vegetation. The ball moss on the Yuccas is an indicator of frequent low clouds and fog. Road continues straight toward the mountains then begins the climb.

5.9 Class 2 road on the climbs: uneven, loose rock, high center, sharp switchbacks and a narrow, one-lane surface requires a sturdy, high-clearance vehicle.

6.6 Photo stop. Canyons drop off at each side of the road. Road is rough as it continues to climb through umber-colored rock.

9.7 Above the fog level at this point the ball moss disappears. Road continues past wide open vistas of surrounding peaks, the area populated with Cardón, Barrel, Cholla and Pitahaya.

12.7 Rancho Los Crestones, on left. Road continues to skirt one deep ravine after another.

16.6 Left up side road to top of hill, photo stop with view to San Ignacio Lagoon, one of the breeding and birthing sites of the California gray whale. Return to road and meet a curve and Cirio forest.

16.7 Trail on left to Rancho Santa Ana.

18.0 Sign: "Pendiente Peligrosa" (Pending Danger). We looked but didn't see much ahead but a good tent site. Because the area is heavily overgrown, much with Cholla, campsites are difficult to find.

18.9 Ranch on left with waterhole, surrounded by towering spires of Cirio.

19.6 Remains of Rancho Los Corralitos. The stone corral area on left appears to be a good clearing for camping on the edge of the rim. Don't be misled. Very often heavy, cold winds in the night will flatten a tent and howl worse than a pack of coyotes, keeping you awake. Camping in the canyon ahead is more comfortable as we learned the hard way. Notice mule trail on left leading into "Gorgeous Gorge."

19.8 Very graphic rock formations in the canyon on the left. We call this "Valley of the Phallus."

21.3 Pinturas Rupestres. The first of the Indian Rock Art sites, *El Ratón*. The site is gated and locked and must be visited with a guide from the village. This 1,100 meter-long cave is thought to have been used by hunters 10,800 years ago. The paintings are at their best in the mornings when the sunlight can reach the recesses of the rock wall.

23.0 The village of San Francisco de la Sierra. The small settlement has a school, church, community building and medical clinic under construction, plus three small markets. Inquire here for a guide to *El Raton* The guides can contact the office in San Ignacio by radio-telephone but at the time of this writing guests wishing to take a mule trip must apply for the permit in person at the office in San Ignacio.

• • • • • • • • • • • • • • • • • • • • • • • • • • • • • • • • • • • •

## Patti's Tip of the Day
Stick an orange or two in your pocket for the mule ride. They're great thirst quenchers.

• • • • • • • • • • • • • • • • • • • • • • • • • • • • • • • • • • • •

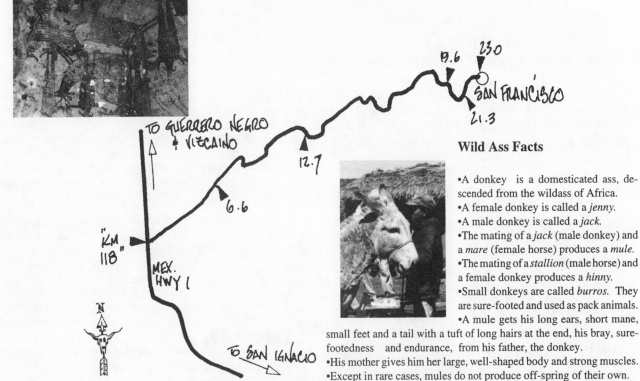

TO GUERRERO NEGRO
& VIZCAINO

"KM 118"

MEX. HWY 1

N

TO SAN IGNACIO

6.6

12.7

19.6    23.0

SAN FRANCISCO

21.3

## Wild Ass Facts

• A donkey is a domesticated ass, descended from the wildass of Africa.

• A female donkey is called a *jenny*.

• A male donkey is called a *jack*.

• The mating of a *jack* (male donkey) and a *mare* (female horse) produces a *mule*.

• The mating of a *stallion* (male horse) and a female donkey produces a *hinny*.

• Small donkeys are called *burros*. They are sure-footed and used as pack animals.

• A mule gets his long ears, short mane, small feet and a tail with a tuft of long hairs at the end, his bray, sure-footedness and endurance, from his father, the donkey.

• His mother gives him her large, well-shaped body and strong muscles.

• Except in rare cases, mules do not produce off-spring of their own.

• The words *mule* and *burro* are spelled the same in English and Spanish but the Spanish pronunciations are, *moo-lay* and *boo-row* .

# SECTION 3
## Mountains, Indians, Missions and Leather

"It is a land of contrast, a land which is utterly incredible, and yet one with such charm that people who go there and once come under its spell are never the same again."

Erle Stanley Gardner
*Off The Beaten Track In Baja*

*Tom keeps saying, "Patti, EVERY back-road trip can't be your favorite." Well, I KNOW that! But this segment of trips starts from our home pueblo of Mulege. From our little casa, we can give you a cup of coffee, load up the trucks and lead you to Cochimi rock art in less than an hour. We can drive you through thick stands of giant Cardon cacti, visit the descendants of the first settlers living in lush ranch country in much the ways of their forefathers. We can get gnarly with rough and rugged trips from the Sea of Cortez over the top of the Sierra de la Giganta moun-*

tain range to one of Baja California's most beautiful and popular surfing beaches on the Pacific. I almost forgot the site of the Misión de Guadalupe, or Misión Santa Rosalía de Mulege at the beginning of one trip, or the very beautiful Misión de San Ignacio. As the surfers say, "Listen up, man, this is adventure!"

To better understand this country let's begin with the Cochimis, the nomadic Indians who inhabited this area long before the Padres began their first exploration and mission settlements. In accounts written by the Jesuit historians, Father Johann Jakob Baegert, from 1751 to 1768, and Father Clavijero in his *History of California,* neither were too enamored with the Baja population. Baegert describes the natives, "Laziness, lying and stealing are their . . . three original sins. They never work, never bother about anything except when it is absolutely necessary to still the pangs of hunger." Father Clavijero wrote that when the first missionaries arrived in Baja they found no huts, pottery, metal instruments or cloth. The people lived on locusts, lizards, caterpillars, spiders and the lice from their hair, plus cactus fruits. They wore minimal or no clothing and were wanderers; yet Father Baegert conceded that although they had nothing, they were always in good spirits and seemed happier than the people back in Europe. The Jesuits, Franciscans, and then the Dominicans labored long and hard to bring these people under the Christian umbrella. Unfortunately, hidden in their good intentions, were the seeds of destruction, the white man's diseases that eventually wiped out every native Baja Californian.

**These ancient dwellers did leave a legacy throughout the peninsula with their rock art paintings.**

We can hike past giant Wild Fig to San Borjitas cave, one of their most dramatic achievements. Here, on a 25-foot high ceiling, these primitive people managed to paint larger-than-life, three-color human and animal figures. Trip 8 could include a side trip to Rancho La Trinidad for a guided hike through one of the valley's loveliest canyons to another rock art site. The more adventurous can continue on, swimming to the other end of the canyon where even more paintings decorate the rock faces. Inquire in Mulege for the local guides.

Padre Nicolas Tamaral gives a more positive description of the Indians than the two previous historians mentioned. He describes them as tall and robust, the women wearing skirts woven from grasses and twigs and skins often painted with figures in bright colors. We also know that they ground seeds or nuts on flat stones called *metates*; unfortunately, many have been scavenged from sites throughout the years, even one that rests on our patio, a gift from a well-intentioned Mexican friend. We've also seen collections of arrowheads of every color and size to know that perhaps in later years, the Indians did considerable hunting. As previously mentioned, on one of our most recent trips a friend stepped out of her truck onto a perfect quartz crystal arrowhead, laying right beside of the road.

Misión Santa Rosalia de Mulege, completed in 1766 by Jesuit Padre Escalante, stands above the fresh water river springing from the ground just west of the town, a lovely beginning to a tour of the countryside. Because of its small "seaport," Mulege became the mission- of- supply with ships arriving here from the Sinaloa and Sonora areas on the Mexican mainland with corn and other necessities. Lovely *a cappella* singing still drifts across the valley when the Padre holds mass. The stone floor, heavy walls and the flicker of candlelight have created romantic settings for several weddings we've attended. Sadly, we buried one of our best friends from this site also. The baptisms of new-borns within the mission walls, complete the life cycles those hard-working Padres must have visualized centuries ago.

The mission trail established a Baja highway of history, dictating the population centers, the food supplies and for the most part, the mores of the citizens.

Although Misión de Guadalupe, a stop on Trip 8, has vanished, the water system and palm trees remain. A modern small block church now stands on the site.

Beginning this mission project in 1720, German Padre Everado Helén received great dedication from the Indians, partly because he studied and learned the Cochimi language. The Chapel of Guadalupe was completed by the next Easter. The mission population suffered terribly in 1722 and 1723 when the peninsula was invaded by a plague of locusts that destroyed planted crops, plus the wild fruits of the pitahaya and other cacti. Although ships at Mulege supplied some corn, the starving Indians began eating the locusts. Many died from dysentery. By 1726, though, Father Helén had a flock of 1,700 Indians living in five surrounding villages. They raised sheep, goats and some crops but even so the land provided only a meager living. In Father Serra's travel north, many years later, he wrote of coming across ten starving families from Guadalupe that the Padre, for lack of food, had been forced to send into the mountains to hunt. He gave what help he could but ultimately, neither Padre Helén's mission nor its Indian inhabitants were able to survive the harsh surroundings.

The descendants of the European soldiers, sent along with the Padres, married native wives and produced a strong, handsome people, known as the *Californios*, the first settlers. Many were deeded thousands of hectares by the King. Bringing knowledge of cultivation and sturdy Spanish cattle, they influenced the off-spring who maintain the prosperous ranches we pass on the backroads today. The Villavicencios and Arces could be described with the three H's: happy, healthy, handsome. You'll meet them and others along the way, appreciate their skill and determination to live well in a sparse and sometimes harsh environment and admire the beauty of their children, the bright-eyed boys and shy girls of the ranch country.

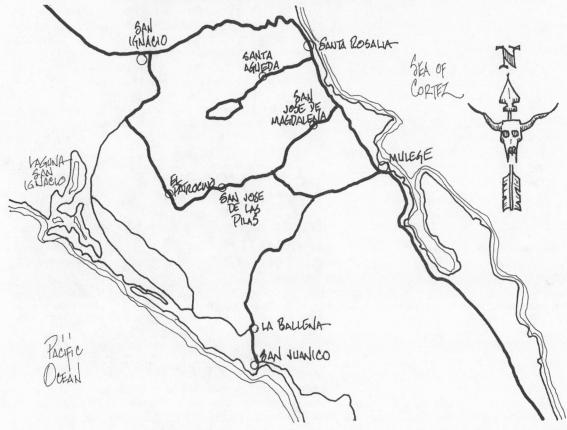

SAN IGNACIO

SANTA AGUEDA

SANTA ROSALIA

SAN JOSE DE MAGDALENA

SEA OF CORTEZ

N

MULEGE

LAGUNA SAN IGNACIO

EL PATROCINO

SAN JOSE DE LAS PILAS

PACIFIC OCEAN

LA BALLENA

SAN JUANICO

# TRIP 8

## The Mulege, Estanislao, San José de Magdalena Loop
(from Mulege west to the mountains and north through the village of
San José de Magdalena to Highway 1 at Km 169)

*"Even in the most rugged parts of the peninsula local
residents spontaneously volunteer their labor to keep
the crude roads in shape. A road is their only
connections with the world, and for them a better
road is a better connection...."*

William Weber Johnson
Baja California

This one-lane graded road travels the hidden Baja of the famous writer, Erle Stanley Gardner. In the early '60's, after hearing of the Indian rock art on the peninsula, he and friends began their visits by specially-built 4 x 4 vehicles and also by helicopter. His books relating his experiences stimulated many an exploration by us "wannabes." Now a road grader has made it possible for us to·visit formerly inaccessible cattle ranches nestled in deep valleys and chat with a vaquero as he passes by on his mule. By chance he may invite us into his *rancho* for a cup of coffee and taste of home-made goat cheese. Without a helicopter we now have the same opportunity as Gardner to sample the isolation and peace of a Baja untouched by Highway 1.

As large signs promise a destination named Estanislao, the one lane road continues ever-nearer a background of cloud-kissed peaks, the

Sierra San Pedro. One section of mesas is a distinctive landmark that identifies the Mulege area from the rest of the coastline when traveling by boat on the Sea of Cortez. The flat tops become close companions as you travel towards the end of the first valley.

Rainfall often turns much of this area into a desert garden, especially in spring when a multitude of Brittlebush borders the roadsides with bright yellow daisies. Farther along, the often dry river beds trickle with water, forming shallow ponds which must sometimes be forded. In spring, scarlet-tipped Palo Adán, a close relative of the Ocotillo, contrast with a carpet of green, yellow and purple ground

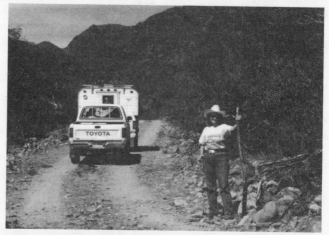

cover. The lemony blossoms of creosote, white-barked Palo Blanco trees, and boulder- strewn flats plus Barrel, Old Man and Organ Pipe cacti survive in aesthetic harmony. The audacity of desert plants is no more evident than the ones that find a smidgen of soil on a rock face and grow to maturity while clinging to an invisible crevice hundreds of feet from the ground.

A marked turnoff leads to Rancho Trinidád, the location of one of the area's rock dams and, more importantly, a spectacular canyon decorated with Indian rock art. When the water warms in the spring, the exploration becomes a wonderful outing with the cooling pleasure of alternately hiking, then swimming the length of the canyon to view the paintings along the canyon walls. To protect the ancient art from vandalism, visitors must be accompanied by a guide who can be hired in Mulege or at the ranch house.

Estanislao, the mysterious destination so well marked with signs, is not a town or village, but rather one of several cattle ranches located in the *sierras*. Once you get off the pavement, there are few population centers, other than ranches, so these backcountry homes are the most easily recognizable landmarks.

*Visitors to Baja often comment on the thin, bony range cattle of the peninsula, especially on the Vizcaino Desert. We sympathize with their listless pace and the Cholla cactus stuck to their faces and haunches. In contrast, the cattle of the Estanislao loop are well-rounded with many healthy calves trailing along. They're so numerous you must watch for them when driving. They also seem much more content. On a recent visit to our friend's ranch, I felt a nudge after getting out of the truck and turned around to be met face to face with a large Brahma bull. I don't know if it was my pink T-shirt or he was in love but he nuzzled me all the way into the gate of the ranch house and Antonio, the owner, had to lock him out. I did learn something with this disconcerting experience. Those large floppy ears are as soft as they appear from a distance and friendly bulls like to have them petted.*

*Later, we stopped at another friend's typical Baja California ranch where Marta was making goat cheese. As usual, the family stopped what they were doing and gathered at our arrival, inviting us into their modest home. Their dirt floors, as always, were swept clean, the folding guest chairs were immediately placed in a circle and we were invited to sit. The offer of coffee always follows their greetings, Siéntese, Siéntese, Como estan? Sit down, sit down, how are you? Mario spoke and one of his young girls brought a large bowl of oranges for us while Marta sent Ana, her teenage daughter, to the stove to begin heating tortillas. Soon they urged us to take places around a small table where Marta and Ana were setting out hot tortillas and a plate of soft curd from the cheese.*

*Warning thoughts about unpasteurized milk vanished quickly as we spooned the soft cream onto the tortillas, adding salt at Mario's urging. Marta's soft cheese tasted better than any supermarket variety, perhaps partly due to our surroundings. Our enthusiasm pleased the family, who, in typical Mexican tradition, did not join us, preferring to stand and watch us eat, ready to serve our every wish.*

*Although this loop trip can be completed in one day, we usually choose to be leisurely, setting up camp in cattle country, deep in this quiet valley rimmed with towering pillars and spires. Quail call to their covey, doves coo, song birds and the tap-tap of a woodpecker play backroad harmony to the soft low of the cattle.*

*As usual, we made camp beneath the twisted boughs of mesquite trees, marvelling at the mature Cholla cacti, taller than a basketball player. Towering mountains on each side of the narrow valley tossed back the echoes of our voices and much later the singing of coyotes.*

*After dark, the moon rose above our campfire through a skyful of puff balls we jokingly referred to as our heavenly sheep. No sooner had we named them than a high breeze decided to play sheepherder. From a point over our heads, "the sheep" fanned out, changing to streaks that radiated out from where we sat at the apex. Backlit by moonlight, with the stars peeking through, the heavens kept us all mesmerized until our stiff necks could take it no longer. Just some more backcountry magic!*

Although Misión Guadalupe has vanished, the site, marked by palm trees and a small block church, is worth a visit. As you walk through the cool shade, a tiny stream of fresh water confirms the reasoning of the German Padre Everardo Helén in choosing this site for a settlement.

From this point the road climbs then dips into deep, sheer-sided canyons. Red peaks streaked with black varnish continue to add drama.

After cruising the Class 1-quality dirt roads through ranch country, this loop drops into one of Baja's loveliest canyons where the condition becomes Class 2. Dramatic rock formations dripping with green vegetation and Wild Fig twist and turn past the one lane road, itself challenging enough to keep the driver interested.

The thick trunks and meandering white roots of the Wild Fig, one of the peninsula's most dramatic trees, is one of the valley's prized sights. With many names, *Higuera, Zalate, Amate, Higuera Silvestre*, the Wild Fig grows slowly, storing water in its huge trunk. The fruit is small and bitter. A tea made from the leaves is used by the ranchers on cattle as an antidote for rattlesnake bite. The ranchers say if a cow is bitten on the lip, the most common area, and they can throw her and force the tea down her throat within two hours of the bite, she will survive. The solution is also used as a poultice on infections and cuts.

Finally, the road descends into the small village of San Jose de Magdalena, known as the garlic capital of Baja California Sur. In season, Magdalena could easily be mistaken for Ireland with the vivid green garlic fields nestled between its craggy background. Each spring, the pueblo marks its patron saint's day with a weekend celebration, sometimes referred to as a garlic festival since the horse races, cockfights and dancing take place at garlic harvest time. Braids of fresh garlic can be purchased in the local stores or directly from the growers A jarring washboard road completes the trip back to the highway, an unfitting finale to the previous excursion. Such scenery needs to be seen, not described.

# TRIP 8

**Trip Length:** 75.1 miles.

**Road Condition:** This road can vary from Class 1 to Class 3, depending on the rainfall and run-off. The ranch country portion can usually be traveled in a high-clearance, sturdy vehicle. The steep portions may require 4-wheel drive. Enjoyable mountain bike and dirt bike trip.
**Supplies and Facilities:**
    **Fuel:** Mulege.
    **Supplies:** Mulege and a small market in S.J. de
              Magdalena.
    **Lodging:** Mulege.

## Trip Log

Mulege west to the mountains and north through the village of San José de Magdalena to Hwy 1.

0.0    Km 36 and Transpeninsular Hwy 1, north of Mulege. Turn off on signed road, "Estanislao 46 Km". Traveling this road, known to locals as "The Ice House Road", you will pass the large building on the right, *Fabrica de Hielo*, the factory where you may purchase block ice. Continue straight through the Mulege suburbs. The road is graded dirt and well-traveled.

2.0    Orange grove ranch on right. Fruit is for sale in season.

2.8    Fork, immediately followed by crossroad. Continue straight.

5.1    IMPORTANT! Fork in road and fence. Water tank on right. **Bear left**.

7.6    Bear right at "Estanislao" sign.

8.3    Another "Estanislao" sign marks a fork of three roads. Take the right fork and pass under the telephone lines.

8.9    Rancho Las Huertas (signed) on left.

12.5   Rancho Las Tinajitas, on left.

12.9   Estanislao sign — "Trinidad, left, Estanislao, 31 Km", straight ahead. Trinidad canyon is the site of Indian rock art. Guides are available at the ranch house adjacent. Follow the signs. It is illegal to visit rock art sites without a guide. Begin the climb through the mountains. Road gets rougher as it travels along canyon on the left. Stream usually has some water flow.

16.0   Rock dam.

20.1   Ranch on left.

20.2   Steep climb. We've done this segment in "Granny Low," without the hubs locked in, but the road was hard-packed at the time. A crude asphalt paving had been added to the steepest portion, helpful at the time of this writing but doubtful in permanence. Sometimes a 2-wheel drive vehicle would have to be towed up this hill. A hard rain definitely changes the conditions.

23.3   Return to the bottom of the wash. After crossing the divide, the water in the streams begins flowing toward the Pacific.

| | |
|---|---|
| 25.0 | Rancho Aguarito, then a fork. (signed) "La Ballena 80", with a left arrow, (see Trip 9); "Estanislao 6, Exmisión Guadalupe 27", with arrow pointing straight ahead. However, the road bears off to the right. All signs in Mexico are in kilometers. |
| 25.8 | Gate. |
| 27.8 | Rancho ESTANISLAO. The stuccoed ranch house speaks of wealth in these parts. The residents are usually very friendly, smiling and waving as you pass by. |
| 38.2 | Rancho Mesquital, on left, well named for the mature mesquite trees growing everywhere. The owners raised seven sons and six daughters on this ranch. Many of the grown children now live on neighboring ranches where they have produced 26 grandchildren for their parents. |
| 38.7 | Gate. |
| 39.4 | San Juan de las Pilas turn-off, to left, signed, (See Trip 10) "Exmisión 6, (arrow straight) S Pedro 21, S J Pilas 32, (arrow left)". Do not be confused by the profusion of roads and signs in this area. Turn RIGHT to go to the mission. The road going straight turns left to S. J. Pilas. At this point we want to emphasize the changes that often take place in these roads, depending on rainfall. The locals often have to make slight changes around washouts or they may grade new roads on higher ground so your mileages may not match the log exactly. The roads that detour will return to the main road again. |
| 45.8 | Site of ex-mission Guadalupe. Nothing remains except the palms. This area is confusing since the road has been diverted since the last hurricane and flooding. Here you will see a palm grove and ranch on the left. Turn back onto a road angling in from the left to a driveway on the right which leads to an old |

ranch. This is the site of the mission. Park and walk up to the ranch buildings and small church.

| | |
|---|---|
| 46.1 | Bear right toward S. J. de Magdalena. Sign, "La Presa", on left. |
| 48.0 | Steep grade, climbing up then skirting the mountains. |
| 49.4 | Steep, loose-rocked downgrade. Very difficult, if not impossible to make it coming up the other way in 2- WD, especially during or just after a rain. This stretch of canyon houses some of the most dramatic examples of Wild Fig on the peninsula. |
| 51.1 | Small ranch with artfully constructed stone wall and corral. |
| 55.5 | Ranch and cattle guard. Road is flat, graded but slow because of river rock base. |

| Mile | Description |
|---|---|
| 56.0 | Rock dam. |
| 57.1 | Mineralized area on right. |
| 61.4 | Sign. "San Sebastian 17, (left) S. J. de Magdalena 7, (right)". |
| 65.4 | The suburbs of Magdalena begin with the power lines and the bright green of the garlic fields, in season. |
| 66.0 | Turn left to *Tienda Rural* store, then stay right through the river bottom.. |
| 66.3 | At the fork go left into what looks like someone's front yard, then stay straight along the old stone wall and orchards on the left. |
| 66.3 | Red-brick store on right. |
| 66.5 | Turn left, wind through the reedy river bottom, then climb the hill to the junction with the graded road that leads to the highway. |
| 75.1 | Transpeninsular Highway 1 at Km 169. |

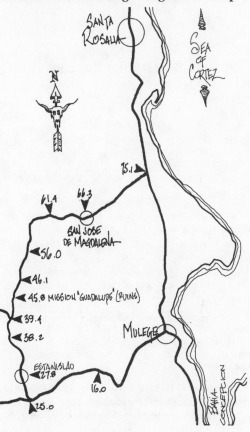

73

## TRIP 9  La Ballena

(25 miles from Mulege to the junction with the Estanislao Road {see Trip 8}, to the destination Rancho La Ballena, then Bahía de San Juanico on the Pacific).

*I'll Admit: "The campfire makes a good cook great."*
*Mike McMahan*
*Adventures in Baja*

Another route from the Sea of Cortez side of the peninsula to the Pacific became an exciting reality when the government cut a new graded road through Arroyo San Ramundo by way of La Ballena. The route starts in the foothills to the west of Mulege and ends on the graded road running parallel to the Pacific coast. According to the government sign at the beginning, the total distance is 80 kilometers, approximately 52 miles. This distance would jibe with the 41.6 miles we have noted above if it hadn't been for Lester.

Lester was a feisty fellow, his surname being Hurricane, who swept across the peninsula in the summer of '92. He wiped out several of the rock dams the government had just then recently installed and destroyed the middle portion of the La Ballena road, making it a true whale of a trip.

When you travel the Baja backroads you learn quickly never to find what you expect. During the planning stage with our friends, Betty and Al, we'd spoken to other friends who had made the trip a couple of

years before in 2WD trucks with no trouble. They had said the trip was tough enough to be interesting but an easy one day over and one day back outing so we decided to include it in a loop trip to San Juanico Bay on the Pacific.

What we forgot? Nothing in Baja can be counted on to be the same as before, even if before was only a month ago. We had also forgotten Hurricane Lester, who changed the course of rivers and central Baja backroading. Ours was a very different trip than our friends' one day excursion.

*The morning of our journey a Mexican rancher friend we'd stopped to see warned us. "Camino muy malo." Very bad road. In the usual practice of the backcountry he'd drawn a line with a stick in the dirt, pointing out the middle section and x'ing it out. Well, Alberto knew his neighborhood and we should have known when a rancher who needs new shocks on his truck after every trip to town, tells you a road is "malo" you can be positive that road is worse than you can imagine.*

*The four of us stood at the crossroads, debating. Betty and Al thought they might just go home early, back to their ranch near Mulege. Tom and I were writing this book and besides wanting to include another sea to ocean route, we couldn't stand not trying. As soon as we said we were going, Betty and Al looked at each other and said, "Why not!"*

*People often shake their heads and ask us what we can possibly like about off-highway adventure. Why would we want to stress our trucks, bump and bounce for hours over trails, sometimes breathe and chew dust or dig it out of our ears and scalp. We find it difficult to explain. There's usually the beauty of raw, unscarred landscapes, or getting to a destination, but much of our pleasure is taking on the unknown because, as I just said, the roads are sometimes not the same as described. Mostly, comes satisfaction in setting a goal and accomplishing what one sets out to do. Betty and Al couldn't go home any more than we would have passed up the turn-off. We all popped a shot of adrenaline and took off, in search of La Ballena.*

Like Alberto's drawing, the road had survived its start and finish but had vanished in-between. Necessity had forced the local ranchers to torture their trucks across a new route, creating a new rugged but passable trail. Much of the time the "road" followed the dry portion of the river bed through the canyon, sometimes fording the stream, sometimes following on its banks.

Tough going doesn't detract from one of the peninsula's loveliest drives, however. The new road passes by palm-lined ponds. Hidden springs in high crevices feed brilliant green vegetation, allowing it to cascade down the dark rock faces of the towering cliffs. Cattle and goats graze while Great White and Great Blue Herons stalk the water for the small fish swimming there. Remote ranches, with cleanly swept yards and brilliant flowers, add to the splendor of their setting.

The ranch folks are very friendly, especially the *vaqueros*, dressed in full leather chaps, riding their mules through the brush. They love to give help, directions and enjoy a cold drink from your cooler. As we were exiting a particularly tricky thicket of low-hanging branches we were surprised to meet a young man coming towards us carrying an ax. A far cry from the Ax Murderer as one might have first suspected, he had heard our vehicles coming and guessed our problem. He'd walked from his ranch to lend a hand in cutting a path, if needed.

This slow, rugged trail is 4-wheel drive recommended. High campers are not recommended because of the many low-hanging branches as the road winds through Mesquite and Palo Verde forests. (Ours has the dents and scrapes to prove it.)

La Ballena was a 1 1/2 day trip for us since much of the trail is taken at a crawl over the river rocks.    One 5-mile segment took us 2 1/2 hours. So what! The Palo Verde trees we passed had showered our hood with yellow blossoms. We camped in a clearing along a stream, and after a full day of tough driving and touching scenery, the campfire quiet sent us to our sleeping bags early.

The La Ballena crossing is worth the effort, a step off the pavement into the lush splendor of mid-Baja California.

Although the Pacific Coast in this area provides many miles of coastline for the backroad explorer with plenty of time, we chose San Juanico as our destination because it is one of our favorite beaches. Just beyond the small fishing village, a wide, smooth beach circles the bay for miles. Many access roads cut out to the sand and if you are careful and have a 4 x 4, or a friend who can get you unstuck, it's possible to camp beach-side with no neighbors.

The people of San Juanico are very friendly. Although their fishing cooperative polices the poaching and selling of illegally caught lobster and abalone, the members very often will GIVE their new-found friends some of their personal supply of seafood. One day a fisherman we had met the day before over a cold beer stopped by and handed us six of the largest abalone we'd ever seen. Then he took them back, and one by one, with the tip of our camping shovel, removed the meat from the shell. Although we invited him and his family to share dinner, we never saw him again. The town has gas, a small store, and one or two restaurants. They seem to change on each visit depending on the mood of the cook. After our spine-shattering drive, Betty and I decided it would be a treat to "go out to dinner." So we stopped at two restaurants to inquire if they were open. Neither were much interested in the idea of us making a reservation to come back at 6:00 for dinner. We'd seen a sign on the way into town for the "Scorpion Bay Campground and Restaurant" so, after a conference, decided to look it over.

A mile or so out of town a newly-constructed *palapa* restaurant overlooks the bay. It sits back from the jagged coastline, partly I suspect, to get away from the strong wind that blows almost every afternoon. The beers were cold, the bartender was friendly and he promised he'd make us a dinner of fresh fish or maybe abalone. Although we remembered these bluffs when they were pristine, without any buildings at all, the purchase and development of the land by three Southern California surfers hasn't destroyed the view.

Bahia de San Juanico, named "Scorpion Bay" by the surfers who've made it famous, at least in their circles, is most popular with the board set from June until November. During the summer months, particularly, a southern swell begins at Punta Pequeña, the farthest point, and skims into Scorpion Bay in perfect right-breaking waves. Five points stretch along the coast for about a mile and a half and Jeff, a friendly guy we met in the *cantina*, swears he, and a few other good surfers, can ride the whole way from the fifth point down into the bay.

We chose a campsite on, I believe, point number three. Jorge, the bartender/manager ran a hose through the window of the women's restroom and hooked it up to an instant hot water heater which was then attached to a shower head. The joyous sensation when warm water pours over your hair and body after several days on the road can only truly be understood by someone who has lived in an unbathed state for more than three days. Like house guests who supposedly stink like fish after three days, backroaders begin to become uncomfortable with themselves after about the same length of time. We all wear caps to camouflage the bad hair days, avoid mirrors and begin to whiff odors better left to ditch diggers. So none of us resented the $3 camping fee that also rented us the use of the showering facilities.

Later, we met another surfer but he gave us a wide berth. Apparently Jeff had told him we didn't speak the language. We thought the "sickest tube" would be "bad, but "bad "means "good" , you know, like "awesome". Let's face it, he knew we were "kooks "who could never "carve it up".

**Trip Length:** 41.6 miles to La Ballena, 14.7 additional to San Juanico.
**Road Condition:** Class 2 and 3. Four-wheel drive recommended. Challenging for dirt bikes. Difficult mountain bike trail because of the river rock. A very slow trip for all.
**Supplies & Facilities:**

      **Fuel:**    Pemex stations at Mulege, from barrels in Ejido Cadeje and San Juanico. Watch for signs when entering the villages. They sometimes have Magna Sin (unleaded gasoline).

**Supplies**: Small market in San Juanico, two restaurants in town, one at campground.
**Lodging**: None.
**Campground**: Yes. Scorpion Bay Campground on the bluffs overlooking the ocean and famous surfing beach. Hot showers. Restaurant, Bar.

# Trip Log
*La Ballena Crossing from the Estanislao Road to San Juanico on the Pacific.*

Follow Trip 8, Mulege, Estanislao, San José de Magdalena, from Transpeninsular Highway 1 at Km 136, north of Mulege for 25 miles to the La Ballena turnoff. See over-all map, Section 3. Start trip log here at 0.0.

0.0     Bear left at Sign: "La Ballena, 80 Km". The road begins as Class 1, smooth, graded gravel but don't be fooled, it will not last.

3.0     On right, the first of many ranches. As a general rule, ignore the roads cutting off left and right and stay on the well-traveled road.

4.4     Neat ranch on right, immediately after the Y. Stay right. Notice the government weather station in the yard, enclosed by chain link fencing. Here you will begin to cross and re-cross the arroyo. Some sections have water over the crossings, some are dry. Unless there has been a recent heavy rain, the crossings are usually shallow and pose no problem. If in doubt, check the depth before attempting to drive through.

6.2     Crossing. Follow sign, R. San Miguel, **bear left**. This is an exception to the rule of following the most-traveled road.

8.5     Rancho San Miguel, on right sits in a wide arroyo, surrounded by towering peaks. Slash left along the road after the grader passed through is available for mesquite campfires.

9.7     Ranch, left, then cross arroyo where unusual rock formations reflect in the pool. Road heads for the sheer faces of the towering mountain fortresses.

10.5    Ranch, right. Heavy rock in the road bed dictates slow speed.

13.5    Fork. Go straight. Continue straight past ranch on left. From here, the road continues to deteriorate, passing through the river bed over cobble and boulders.

15.8    Goat ranch, on right. The road narrows to a trail. Many low-hanging branches and tight brush. Necessary to keep windows closed at times to prevent injury to passengers from branches and thorns. The drive continues at creeping speed over a rock-filled trail. My notes read, *"Muchas Piedras. Muy malo!"* (Many rocks. Very bad!)

18.4    Narrow, sharp turns and more river bed to cross. The roughness of the road, forcing slow speed, dictates the opportunity to really observe the diverse desert vegetation.

20.0    Y in road. Ranch on left. Stay right through a fantastic forest of old, gnarled mesquite.

21.7    A surprise marshland. Reeds grow along the shore, ducks swim and a Great White Heron stalks his prey in the shallow water.

22.2    Ranch on left. Y in the road, bear left.

23.7    Y in road, bear right down into a palm-studded arroyo.

24.8    Road is difficult to follow since everything around is river rock. Don't go to the ranch. Stay in stream bed, skirting the edge of the low mesa, then ford back to other side.

25.8    Excellent camp spot beside river with view of river, reeds, herons and ducks.

26.3    Pass ranch then road becomes sand with less-dense brush. Much easier going except for low branches.

29.4    Road turns left. Graded road begins.

30.2    Road climbs to top of mesa then drops down into another palm-shaded Shangri-la along the river. Another mile and you ford the stream again.

34.2    Y in road, bear right. Note the change to dry desert with low vegetation and very few trees except in the washes.

40.6    Road turns and crosses to north side of the river bed.

41.6    At the crossroad, turn left. The orange ranch house on the left at the Km 10 marker is

RANCHO LA BALLENA!

Pass the ranch, climb the hill and take the left fork. You are back to uninteresting graded, gravel road punctuated with washboarding. The scenery changes to dry desert with little vegetation. This stretch of graded gravel Class 1 road is a way to get from point A to B quickly, not the scenic route.

47.7    Ejido Cadeje, a small village. Fuel is usually available from barrels, watch for sign on left. A surcharge is added for the service. Both Nova (leaded, regular) and Magna Sin (unleaded) are usually available.

56.3    Enter San Juanico, gas station on right. In town, turn right on any street to Scorpion Bay campground. Continue straight to the beaches along the bay and La Purisima.

## "La Ballena" A "Whale" of A Trip !

### No-Mess-Dinner in a Packet

On each 12-inch square of heavy-duty foil, slice one potato, one onion, 1/2 green pepper and one small zucchini. Add one hamburger patty or two slices of Spam. Season with salt and pepper. Add one Tbsp margarine to vegetables.

Form into a flat packet and seal with double folds. Grill over gray coals for approximately 30 minutes, turning every 5 minutes. Cooking time will vary depending on heat and distance from the coals.

We dig a shallow pit next to our campfire and transfer the hot coals into it for better control of the cooking temperature.

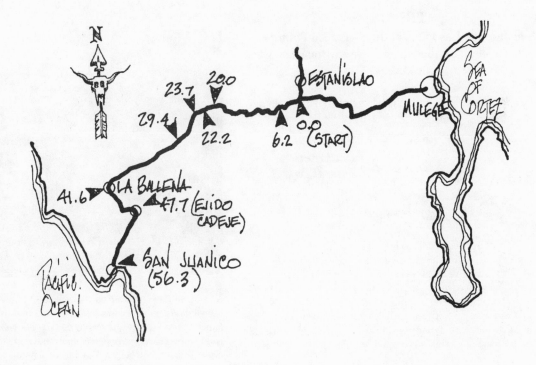

N

29.4

23.7   20.0

22.2

ESTANISLAO

MULEGE

SEA OF CORTEZ

6.2   0.0 (START)

41.6   LA BALLENA

47.7 (EJIDO CADEJE)

SAN JUANICO (56.3)

PACIFIC OCEAN

# TRIP 10
## San Juan de Las Pilas, in the Sierra La Palmita
### (Between San Ignacio Lagoon Road & Estanislao, west of Mulege)

*"Judgement and luck are still a big part of Baja travel and maybe it's that spice and tingle of worry that keeps pulling gringo adventurers back."*

Jim Hunter
*Offbeat Baja*

"The River Rock Trail" is not for the faint-hearted. This is a trip for the frustrated, those who missed driving the length of Baja in the 40's. If you've read Erle Stanley Gardner's account of his backcountry adventures and yearned to see "the other Baja," then this is your chance.

Warnings are in order, however. This trail is definitely for 4x4s and dirt bikes. Not recommended for mountain bikes. The equipment should be sturdy and in good condition. Travel with a buddy since help in case of a break-down could be miles and hours away.

*We were miles off the Transpeninsular highway on a Mulege to San José de Magdalena trip, (see Trip 8) when we first saw the government sign for San Juan de Las Pilas, 32 kilometers. From the*

*ranch country we started up the mountain road which quickly became narrow and very steep. Being alone, without another vehicle, we turned back, determined to get there another time and find out where the route would exit. The topographical maps showed no through route. Months later we were traveling into San Ignacio Lagoon, and there it was again, a government sign pointing to Las Pilas. We'd found the other end of the road!*

*On another day with our friends, Betty and Allen, we returned to San Ignacio to begin our adventure — and adventure it was. To see some of the most dramatic Baja backcountry to be found, we drove miles and miles through the bottom of a dry river bed. The privilege of viewing canyons washed by time into crevices and caves or a mountainside dripping with palm trees and vivid green vegetation required hours of twisting and turning through miles of truck- and bone-jarring river rock. The adventure does not end there, however. It finishes with a roller-coaster-twisting climb up to the crest of the mountain, where on a clear day you can see both the Pacific Ocean and the Sea of Cortez. Then comes the thrilling descent into a valley of lush ranch country. One grade approaches 15% straight down (or up, depending on your direction); just the sight of it starts the adrenaline flowing.*

*On this passage you have the chance to meet the rancheros who live in isolation, satisfied to ride their mules to "San José," as they call San José de Magdalena, the nearest village, to replenish their stores every month or two. It's usually the Dons, the older members of the ranch families, who you'll see decked out in their finest leathers — tooled boots, saddle and chaps — riding the road to town, with an empty saddlebag, herding as many as five or six other pack animals along. As these handsome pioneers pass by with a cheerful "Adios," you know you've not only gone backroad but also back in time.*

**Length of Trip:** 59.4 miles.

**Road Condition:** Mostly Class 3, driving much of the time in river bed over large, uneven rock. 4-wheel drive vehicle and dirt bikes recommended. *Very* rugged for mountain bikes.

**Supplies & Facilities:** None.

## TRIP LOG
*Between San Ignacio Lagoon Road & Estanislao, west of Mulege.*

| | |
|---|---|
| 0.0 | San Ignacio. Begin in front of the mission in the town square. Turn left around the square, pass bank on left, continue straight through the residential section of town. |
| 0.3 | Turn right. Pass *Delegación* building. |
| 0.4 | Immediately turn left at microwave dish. ( Here you will see a red SCORE arrow on a stone wall — a little American graffiti left over from the Baja 1000!) A government sign gives kilometers to La Laguna 59 and S. Juan de Las Pilas 98. Pass through the dump. |
| 3.0 | Interesting arena rimmed with used tires on left. The road is hard and rocky, rough on gear and passengers. Sand roads run parallel; although no faster because of dips and unexpected rocky areas but they are more comfortable. |
| 5.9 | Rancho Bateque. Severe washboard in this area. |
| 8.3 | Rancho San Joaquin with palms and fruit trees. |
| 9.7 | Note the " living fence" of yucca posts on right. |
| 10.7 | Rancho Conafe. |
| 12.5 | San Zacarias, a small community with a tiny market. Last chance to buy forgotten staples. |
| 18.7 | Turn-off to S.J. de Las Pilas. Signed: "El Patrocino 35, S. J. de Las Pilas 66". In miles, about 44. The road is rocky and rough, 5 mph. |
| 24.7 | Upgrade to a 25-mph stretch before traveling downhill into the arroyo. Ford a stream bed. |

| | |
|---|---|
| 28.6 | Ranch on left . Take the road bearing to the right. |
| 29.3 | Begin steep climb into mountains. Rough with sharp rocks. Then the road runs straight across a Joshua tree-filled valley. |
| 38.2 | Ranch on left. An oasis of palms, fruit trees and garden. Three more ranches follow. |
| 41.4 | Rancho El Patrocino (signed). Tiny blue church on right, ranch on left with fenced-in government weather station. |
| 43.3 | Fork. Stay left and climb hill. |
| 46.6 | Keep going straight ahead. Rough, creeping progress over boulders. |
| 50.5 | Downgrade of loose rock. *Came upon two girls riding burros.* This is slow going. *Burros are faster than trucks.* |
| 51.8 | Ranch. Road turns down into river bed. ROUGH! |
| 52.4 | Up again, through lovely steep-walled canyon. |
| 53.4 | Gate. Be sure to re-close and re-tie. Road crosses back and forth across the river bed through steep canyon walls streaked with dark varnish. |
| 54.9 | Gate and palm trees. |
| 55.1 | Ranch. (My log here reads, "A patchwork quilt of rocks and plants. Umber and varying hues of green background appliqued with giant Candalabra Cactus.") As the road crosses the river bottom, you come upon pools alive with polliwogs. |
| 57.6 | Gate. |
| 58.6 | A majestic Wild Fig with roots descending approximately 50 feet down the canyon wall to the ground. |
| 60.5 | SAN JUAN DE LAS PILAS! This lush green ranch with palms, saddles straddling the fence, goats and the beginning of a stone aqueduct paralleling the road is a welcome destination point, although getting there is really the goal. The road continues through more lush landscape where palms and vines |

cliff-hang from their spring-fed water source alongside caves and balancing rocks.

| | |
|---|---|
| 61.5 | Another Wild Fig with cascading roots stands guard over two cave paintings. Look but don't touch. Farther along, the sunlight on rippled pools sends dancing lights across the tops of cave ceilings. |
| 62.1 | CAUTION. The road begins to climb. One very sharp turn to the right is impossible to make without backing up and going forward a few times. This is on a steep incline of loose rock, use care. After the climb, the road moves away from the canyon. |
| 63.4 | Gate. Be sure to close and re-fasten all gates. |
| 65.5 | Ranch on right. |
| 65.9 | Ranch on left. |
| 68.6 | IMPORTANT! Fork. Bear right. Contrary to the usual back-road travel, the left road shows more travel but is not the through road. |
| 69.4 | Closed gate (Camping near here, we were visited by Señor Rosas from the next ranch. This gentleman is a licensed guide and conducts mule/burro trips in the surrounding mountains to see the Indian rock art. He invites passersby to visit his ranch where he is quite proud of the federal guide permit issued to him in 1976). |
| 70.1 | Fork. Right goes to the ranch. This is Rancho Sauca Rosas. The area is San Pedro de La Sierra. The road from Las Pilas toward Estanislao shows more maintenance and use. From here you will begin a climb to the top of the mountain. The road is narrow and steep with many switchbacks. The extreme degree of ascent requires caution. Low gear recommended. |
| 73.6 | THE TOP! From here, on a clear day, you can see the Pacific Ocean AND the Sea of Cortez. There is plenty of room to pull |

off and park.

75.5 WARNING! An extremely steep, downgrade will be coming up. The locals have paved the steepest portion of the incline to make it somewhat passable. Use your lowest gear and brake as little as possible. Although it looks as if you will fall off the edge of the earth at the bottom, there is plenty of room to stop and park if you want to give thanks at the small shrine another passerby has erected in a cardboard box. You've been there! You've done it!

77.0 Fork. Bear left. Sign, viewed from opposite direction, "S.J. de Las Pilas 26".

79.3 Fork. Bear right to Estanislao and Mulege. Left goes to Misión Guadalupe and S. J. de Magdalena.

## Trip 10 MAP  San Juan de Las Pilas, The River Rock Trail

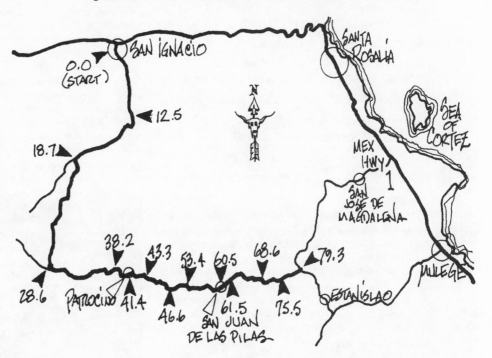

# TRIP 11
## Santa Agueda & Candelaria

*"In our complex civilization we are whipped into an artificial rapidity of pace which strains our nerves to the limit. But down in Baja California one suddenly sees things in a new perspective."*

Erle Stanley Gardner
*Hovering Over Baja*

The small village of Santa Agueda was established by the French in the 1880's to supply nearby Santa Rosalía and its copper mining operation with fresh water. Beyond, the road travels through a lovely valley dotted with ranches.

The families, residing only 20-plus miles from the blacktop and the fair-sized town of Santa Rosalía, still live mostly in the old ways of their forefathers: without electricity, raising cattle and goats to provide dairy products, meat, and the leather for shoes and saddles. Their ranches also support lovely gardens and orchards, heavy with fruits, blooming with flowers and happy faces.

On our last visit, our friend Francisco, a goat rancher, led us through his amazing shoe-making process. We examined his tanning vats. Made from the skin of a cow, the hide is stretched over a frame of wood sitting atop sturdy, home-made legs. The cowhide vat is then filled with water and bark chips from the Palo Blanco tree. Goat skins are scraped of fur and fat, dried, then tanned in this mixture. Francisco cuts the leather into the pieces he needs to make shoes for the family. Known to the ranchers as tehun, the type of footwear he creates resembles what we used to call "desert boots", a low hiking boot-style with laces and sturdy truck-tire soles. (See Trip 7A). This is the footwear of choice for the vaqueros of the backcountry rather than the western boots we're used to seeing on cowboys. The men say the soles give better traction, are more comfortable, inexpensive and impervious to cactus spines..

Santa Agueda rests in a canyon of lush desert vegetation where the abundance of water has transformed even the usually sparsely-leafed Palo Adáns into green, leafy trees. Every plant in this canyon, like the people, seems to be in a state of perpetual well-being.

On our most recent trip, we traveled to the end of the road where, from a distance, Rancho Las Higueras sits at the base of the towering mountains like a lone tomato in a bowl of green salad. The panorama of green against varnished, sheer cliffs creates a soul-satisfying image. This ranch, and most of the valley, are owned by the Villavicencios, one of the oldest Baja families. Their ancestor was said to be a tall soldier, born in Guadalajara, who arrived in Loreto in 1732 at the time of Jesuit rule; the men of the family, like him, are tall and handsome.

After admiring the lovely setting and the ranch house ablaze with blooming flowers, we passed on to Rancho La Candelaria where the eldest of the family has lived beneath the towering mountains for 70 years in a house that's a centenarian. From Rancho Candelaria it's a 45-minute walk to visit rock art done by the ancient people of Baja many centuries before the Villavicencios arrived. A guide is usually available.

**Trip Length:** 53 miles, round-trip.
**Road Condition:** Class 1 to Santa Agueda, then mostly Class 2. Small stretches of Class 3 in Candelaria area. Auto or motorhome to Santa Agueda. Remainder: sturdy 2 WD okay, except last miles to Candelaria area where 4-wheel drive vehicle is recommended. An interesting mountain bike or dual-purpose motorcycle trip.

**Supplies and facilities:**
**Fuel**: No.
**Supplies**: Small market in Santa Agueda for staples. For lengthy stay, shop in Santa Rosalía.
**Lodging**: None.

## Trip Log
### *Hwy 1 at Km 189 to Santa Agueda & Candelaria*

0.0     Highway 1 at Km 189, 1/4 mile south of the Santa Rosalía prison. A sign for "Ramal A Santa Agueda", marks the turn-off onto a Class 1 hard-surfaced gravel road with only minor washboarding.

7.0     The village of Santa Agueda with the school directly ahead. Turn left and continue down the main street. Past town the road begins to deteriorate into Class 2. Autos and motorhomes should not continue.

8.2     At this rough down-grade into the valley, the road begins to deteriorate, with more loose rock, minor wash-outs and narrowing to one lane.

11.6     Rancho El Bule, the first of several well-maintained ranches, appears on the right. The original adobe homestead is still in evidence.

11.9     Plan a picnic here under the boughs of three Wild Fig trees.

15.6     San Javier Ranch, on the left, white picket fence and satellite dish.

19.2     El Tajo, a beautiful ranch with palms and flower gardens. The mountains, closer now, show off their peaks and sheer faces of polished patina dripping with varnish.

21.6     Blue painted rocks lead up hill, on left, to small shrine, newly plastered and painted at our last visit.

22.7     Santa Rosa. This is an important fork in the road. Here the signs can be misleading with the top sign reading, "Rcho La Higueras," the one under it reading, "La Candelaria 8 km" (with an arrow pointing right, leading you to think that Higueras is left, Candelaria, is right.) Wrong! Both ranches are to the right, (see map). The road to the left leads off into the mountains. Turn right. Continue straight to the foothills and the beautiful Rancho Las Higueras, a plant lover's paradise. From the Santa Rosa fork, the remainder of the trip is definitely Class 3 with more loose rock, rougher surface, and tougher grades. A 2-wheel drive, heavy-duty vehicle can probably make it but 4-wheel drive alleviates the spinning and slipping of tires and stress to both vehicle and driver.

25.4     Rancho Las Higueras. A road turns right toward La Candelaria.

26.7     Rancho La Candelaria. Here you can inquire for a guide or directions to the rock paintings. It's possible and interesting to make this portion of your exploration a circle trip by taking a second road (see map) back to Santa Rosa.

● ● ● ● ● ● ● ● ● ● ● ● ● ● ● ● ● ● ● ● ● ● ● ● ● ● ● ● ● ● ● ● ● ● ● ● ●

### Patti's Tip of The Day
Although gifts are not necessary on visits to the ranches, the ladies enjoy skin cream and flower seeds and the children love stuffed animals or balloons.

● ● ● ● ● ● ● ● ● ● ● ● ● ● ● ● ● ● ● ● ● ● ● ● ● ● ● ● ● ● ● ● ● ● ● ● ●

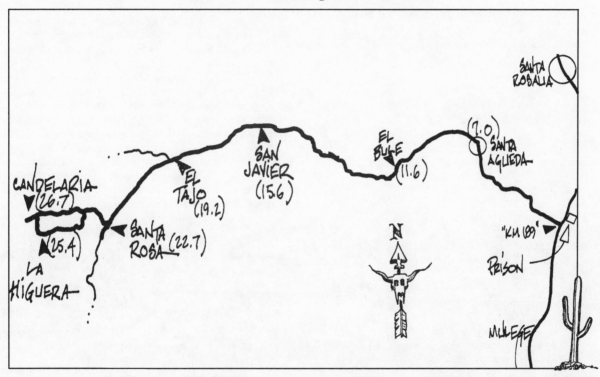

# SECTION 4
## By the Sea, The Beautiful, Bountiful Sea

### Reflections of a Tide Pool

*Determined, nervous crabs,*
*Kick up clods of wet sand,*
*In their haste to escape intruders.*
*Confused seashell dwellers,*
*Draw useless scribbles.*
*The plodding snails in no hurry,*
*Like us,*
*Some have goals, some fall short,*
*Some will perish ,*
*Before the next tide.*

*The remote beaches of the Sea of Cortez are like that. They inspire introspection even at the risk of writing bad poems. Their isolation begs the senses to awaken — to look, listen, think, feel.*

The drives to all of the beaches in this section are as much fun as being there. Since the easiest route to anywhere in Baja is often through an *arroyo*, many of the backroads of the peninsula go through canyons rather than over hills. The Indians and then the settlers chose these routes for ease, surely, more than for their beauty, but loveliness is the reward for a sometimes bouncy ride. Trees and plants of the *arroyos* enjoy what run-off arrives with each rain and grow more luxuriously than their plains counterparts. Palo Blanco, Palo Verde and Wild Fig shade the canyons while rock faces give life to vines or an occasional Barrel cactus.

History tells us these beaches were occasional destinations on the Indian trail and a Cochimí undoubtedly picked up a shell or ate a raw crab or ant on this same sand. An explorer sent out by the Padres in Loreto in the early 1700's might have felt the same satisfaction when he sailed into Bahía San Basilio as the backroader of today feels when he successfully reaches the beach. He probably rowed ashore to gather clams or search for pearls. And the seagulls surely squawked just as loudly at the disturbance of their beach or moved closer hoping to snatch a snack.

*The beaches of the Sea of Cortez create permanent mental images, some imagined, some real. Picture the violent upheaval of nature when the volcanic offshore islands first appeared. Imagine hot, molten lava pouring down surrounding mountainsides. A pod of dolphin break the glassy morning sea in a slow motion water ballet. Suddenly a whale spouts in the distance. Cottony clouds reflect a mirror image on the water; a string of pelicans glides by, near enough to hear the pumping of wings.*

*The beaches of the Sea of Cortez don't request your presence but if you come they will provide an outstanding performance, unique each time.*

## CLAMS AT THE BEACH

When the butter or chocolate clams are fresh from digging, grab a knife, a lemon, a bottle of Tabasco, and eat them raw. If that isn't your thing then toss them on the barbecue grill over hot coals. They will begin to sizzle and steam in the shell. As they pop open, hand them out to be eaten from the shell with a squeeze of juice and a drop or two of hot sauce.

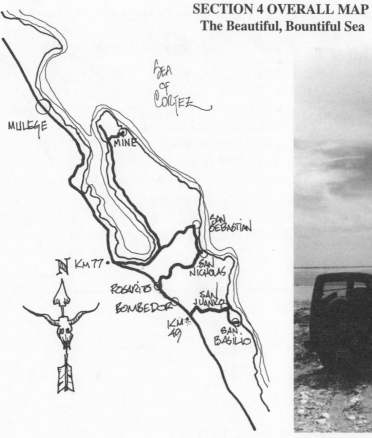

90

# TRIP 12
## THE OTHER SIDE OF CONCEPCION BAY
### (South of Mulege, at Km 77+)

*"The ultimate dream of every true beachcomber is a gently curving beach, remote and uninhabited and generously stocked with man's debris and nature's discards. Baja has it!"*

Ginger Potter
*BAJA BOOK IV*

Twenty-eight mile-long *Bahía Concepción* is probably the Baja Peninsula's most popular beach camping mecca. With sandy beaches flanking its length, most of the year RVs and tents nestle up beside thatch-roofed palapas all along the side of the bay you see when traveling down Highway 1. If you leave the pavement at the south end of the bay, however, and travel the dirt to "the far side" you will meet a different breed of bay. The sandy beaches are fewer and so are the rigs. The desert varies from sparce to lush and thick. Hawks and frigates hang out on the tops of the Cardón, watching the quiet life of the desert. The road varies from smooth flats to washboard to rough rock with little elevation change until the crossover to the Sea of Cortez side at the tip. Most of the way can be traveled by 2WD or bikes, or even a tough auto in dry weather. There are several hills that could trick the unwary with ruts and rock. Four-wheelers will find the entire trip a breeze.

The rainbow at the end of the drive is multi-hued with a pot of exploratory rewards awaiting visitors. Deserted sandy beaches, perfect for camping and swimming, share the shore with rocky underwater reefs where Parrot and Angelfish add their colors to the scenery.

A manganese mine built during World War II, then abandoned is worth a walk around. Although little of the mine remains except the concrete structures, scavengers may find a rusted cooking skillet or a tin lantern left by the Mulege villagers and their families who lived there for the short time the mine was in operation. Panchon, a waiter in Mulege, was born in this temporary settlement. A cemetery on the hill gives evidence that although some babies were born on this remote point of Baja, a few lives also ended.

During the many years we have poked around the backcountry of Baja, we have encountered rattlesnakes only twice, both times while exploring or camped in the mine area or in the brush area at the end of this drive; so be careful. Rattlers have excellent protective coloring making them difficult to see and contrary to common belief, they do not always rattle. The one our friend, Allen, almost stepped on never made a peep. But neither did he strike so take this as a warning to watch where you walk, not as a reason not to visit.

**Trip Length:** 53 miles, round-trip.

**Road Condition:** Mostly Class 2 in dry weather. This drive not recommended in wet or rainy weather. Some areas subject to flooding and mud. Interesting mountain bike ride with many beach camping sites available along the way. Many hiking trails.

**Supplies & Facilities:** None.

## TRIP LOG

0.0    Turn off from Highway 1 south of Mulege, just past Km 77 at the end of the bay. A deserted government campground can be seen at the edge of the water. This concentration camp-style compound was built at the time the Transpeninsular highway was completed but never opened. As is evident, the area is also subject to flooding in rainy season and also at very high tides. The road is smooth when dry but can be very slick with sticky mud even after a light rain.

4.7    Washboarding begins. Because of flooding at times, you will see many alternate routes angling off to higher ground. Most return to the main road quickly.

5.4    Fork, stay left. The first tree you see on the right is "The Love Connection." If you look closely, it's actually a pair, one mesquite and one Jito tree, entwined in each other's arms. Passersby have left romantic and sometimes graphic graffiti carvings in the bark.

5.5    Fork. Stay left down into an arroyo. ( The right fork continues to San Sebastian cove, on the Sea of Cortez. Trip 13). Continue towards the water, past a tumble of volcanic rock on the right. Mounds of scallop shells attest to the abundant bloom and harvest of bay scallops a few years back.

6.4    Road meets shoreline. This portion can be wet at high tide but usually passable. The buoys in the water off-shore are a part of a scallop re-planting project, still in the experimental stage.

6.9    Fish camp, often deserted.

8.4    One of many arroyos with hiking trails leading to the hills.

8.9    Arroyo.

9.9    "The Three Musketeers" arroyo, guarded at the entrance by three tall Cardón, which on approach seem to be barring the road. A good campsite.

13.2    Rancho Margarita, on the water.

14.4    A road goes off to right to Los Carapachos, posted private property.

16.9    Fork. Take either as they rejoin later.

23.7    Rancho. Signed: "Whit's End, The Far Side."

28.8    Upgrade. Rocky and chopped up, rough road bed and some deep potholes. Could be tough for 2-wheel drive.

30.2    Fork. Left to Santo Domingo Bay with a sand beach for camping and shelling. Turn right to continue on to the other side of the peninsula and the abandoned mine.

31.8    Rutted downgrade, use care.

34.5    Beach area. A road goes over the hill to the north, then down to the beach. Park here and hike north to the mine site.

# MAP FOR TRIPS 12 AND 13

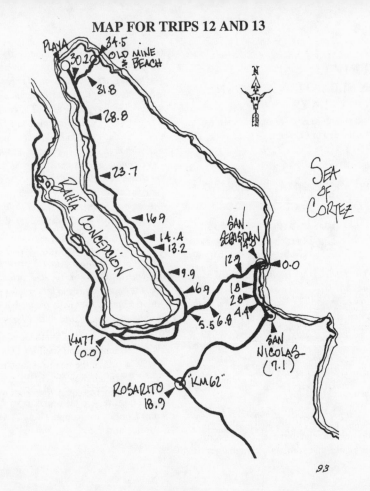

PLAYA

34.5
OLD MINE
& BEACH
30.2

31.8

28.8

23.7

16.9

14.4
13.2

9.9

6.9

5.5 6.8

BAHIA CONCEPCION

N

SEA OF CORTEZ

SAN SEBASTIAN
14.8

12.9

0.0

1.8

2.8
4.4

KM 77
(0.0)

SAN NICOLAS
(7.1)

ROSARITO
18.9

"KM 62"

# TRIP 13
## LOOP TRIP: SAN SEBASTIAN AND SAN NICOLAS BAYS

(South of Mulege and Bahía Concepción, at Km 77+ on Transpeninsular Hwy 1 to San Sebastian Cove on the Sea of Cortez, then to San Nicolas, returning to Hwy 1 at El Rosarito)

Then the sea
And heaven rolled as one and from the two
Came fresh transfigurings of freshest blue.

Wallace Stevens
*Sea Surface Full of Clouds*

The 14-mile off-pavement drive from Highway 1 at the south end of Bahía Concepción to San Sebastian Cove on the Sea of Cortez was one of our first Baja backcountry experiences. Friends escorted us the first time. We stopped at the ranch just adjacent to the cove and visited with Cipriano, the one-legged goat rancher, his sister, and niece. The women were so shy we barely saw them, except when Cipriano poured the tequila our friends had brought for him. More than a decade ago the small cove was deserted except for a few fishermen who camped out on the south end of the shore and anchored their pangas in the protected harbor.

Since they were out fishing and rarely at home, we and our traveling companions had the place to ourselves -- except for the pigs.

On our first camp-out we found out why the cove was nicknamed, "Bay of Pigs." In the night we were invaded by a herd of the rancher's pigs who managed to open our food chest and root out and eat everything of value, while making a paste of pancake flour and cooking oil which they smeared on everything else. The cove has changed with the invasion of the "gringos." A few intrepid souls have towed in trailers and imported lumber and cement to build permanent structures which ring the cove and, although the rocky shore is available for camping, we now feel we're camping in someone's front yard.

The drive, though, is still rough enough to make one feel adventurous as the road travels through some of Baja's more spectacular stands of Cardón and forests of graceful Palo Blanco. We always stop to trace the meandering roots of a mature Wild Fig as it clings to the side of a sheer bluff.

Although we regret the changes that have taken place at the end of the road, the trip is still worth the drive, to stop by the ranch and visit with long-time resident Cipriano and his niece, Manuela, then go on to the beach hoping to hit the tide pools at low tide. There's also good fishing from the rocks and from what we've seen, the "new natives" are friendly and don't mind a little intrusion into their quiet lives. This short, tough drive is more comfortable at a slow pace in 4-wheel drive but is driven regularly by high clearance 2-wheel drive trucks.

Four-wheelers can have the extra thrill of completing a loop with the next trip, continuing to San Nicolas, then back out to the highway.

**Trip Length:** 24 miles round trip.

**Road Condition:** Rough, Class 2. Great dirt bike trip.

**Supplies and Facilities:** None.

# LOG
## *To San Sebastian*

0.0   Turn east off Hwy 1 at Km 77+.

5.5   Fork. Stay right to San Sebastian. Left goes the length of the bay to an old mine on the shore of the Sea of Cortez (See Trip 12). Road is typical hard pack, comfortable except for some washouts and loose rock.

6.8   Road dead ends. Take road left into bottom of arroyo. Rough section begins with uneven, loose upgrades. The rocks show the signs of tire rubber from skidding. Preferable in 4 x 4.

10.4  Tricky spot after a rain. Here the canyon narrows and the road passes through a forest of Palo Blanco. The bark from this tree is used by the ranchers to tan their cow and goat hides. As the hills become cliffs, the rocky river bed continues to jostle vehicles and passengers. A slow crawl is best to prevent damage to the truck undercarriage.

12.9  Plenty of space to pull off the road and stop to enjoy the shade of the Wild Fig, on right.

13.0  Fence marks entrance to the ranch property.

13.6  Old Ranch.

13.7  Cipriano's ranch house in the palm grove. He welcomes visitors.

14.0  Arrive at beach.

# LOG
## *San Sebastian To San Nicolas and Highway 1 at El Rosarito, Km 62*

0.0   Restart Log at Cipriano's ranch house. Take road on the beach-side of the house, south. WARNING! The road climbs and turns a very sharp BLIND curve. The driver's side is a very steep drop-off. The road is narrow with loose rock. Since, because of the incline, the driver cannot see where the road goes around the curve, he must hug the right bank as closely as is possible. After this "Not for the Faint-Hearted" curve, the road climbs then drops down to the bluffs overlooking the Sea of Cortez. The scenery is spectacular with many sites suitable for camping.

1.8   After a steep downgrade into the *arroyo*, a road runs left to a rocky shore. The tidepools in this small cove stay uncovered much of the time, unless there is a very high tide. The water

*95*

caught in some of the basins catches the rays of the sun to provide a warm tub. A good campsite.

1.9 A steep, rough upgrade climbs back to the top of the bluffs and the sea scenery. Punta Pulpito can be seen off to the east. A series of narrow, sharp switchbacks begin.

2.8 Begin a steep downgrade that would be even more challenging from the reverse direction.

3.0 Down to the water and Romarita fish camp. The road continues another series of breathtaking climbs, drops and curves. It's a fun road!

4.4 This is a "must" stop for the primo view of the drive. From the palisade you can look down into "fish city" below. The residents swim in and out of the seaweed and around the reef. The Sea of Cortez spreads its ragged shores like crusts of wheat bread, while a wayward crumb, Isla San Ildefonso, floats offshore. The road continues to deliver a roller coaster ride, up and down, to and above the sea.

5.6 Fish camp with permanent housing.

7.1 Main road into San Nicolas. Turn left to village. Right goes to Highway 1. A sign at this junction asking you to carry out your trash gives an indication of the pride which is apparent in the village. The road left passes neat ranches and leads to the school and attractive stuccoed church.

8.0 Sandy beach, fishing *pangas* pulled up here. Return to fork and take main road to El Rosarito. This road begins as Class 1, graded gravel that appears to be a 40 mph road. But there are many dips that sneak up and could cause your vehicle damage if hit at high speed.

18.9 Junction. Transpeninsular Hwy 1 at Km 62 at the village of El Rosarito.

# TRIP 14
## San Juanico Cove and Playa San Basilio
### (Between Mulege and Loreto at Km 49.)

"...I sincerely believe that the Baja peninsula is magnificent."

Jack Williams
*The Magnificent Peninsula*

Solitary walks with damp sand massaging the toes encourages one to breathe in heavily of air seasoned with salt.

A psychedelic experience occurs with a swim at night in the phosphorescence made by microscopic organisms. Any movement produces a shower of star-fire that combines with the heavens above to create the sensation of swimming through stars. Snorkeling through the tiny yellow and black bodies of a thousand or more baby Sergeant Majors or casting a line and catching a dinner of sea bass or grilling hot dogs around the campfire with your friends are all experiences of monumental importance on a beach beside the Sea of Cortez.

The "yachties" sailing the Sea of Cortez stop regularly in San Juanico Cove, appreciating its shelter and beauty so much they have even created a shrine. What began as a few visiting boats leaving a simple memento, has evolved into elaborate wind chimes and wood and sandstone carvings of the yacht name and date of visit. A walled area under a tree has become an interesting history of the area's boating activity. *The wide bay and its companion bay to the north, San Juanico, protect some of the sea's most attractive beaches and coastal rock formations.*

*Until a few years ago, the boat people had the snorkel-perfect San Juanico Cove to themselves. Now a road exists and with it: Baja backroad explorers. To the chagrin of some, too many backroad explorers means a lack of privacy and that "all to myself" feeling of being able to have a beach to yourself. Most times, though, you can find a beach to be alone — or you discover neighbors who become friends.*

*The road into San Juanico fish camp has been around for some time and when the fishing is good, the* panga *fishermen also set up camps in the coves, so a sharing, like it or not, is sometimes necessary.*

*The off-highway drive to the beaches should be as enjoyable as the destination. The road passes through a typical arroyo environment, luxuriant with vegetation. Forests of Palo Verde bloom gold in the spring, while the black and white branches of the Palo Blanco seem to reach out eerily as you pass by, like the animated spooks in a Disney movie. In some places, the side of the road looks more like cotton fields, puffy with the soft bloom of Desert Lavender.*

*The coves are ideal for small boating, fishing, boardsailing, kayaking and diving.*

*The drive in, and the destination, invite both newcomers and returnees.*

**Length of Trip:**  10.9 miles from Km 49 on Transpeninsular Hwy 1.

**Road Condition:**  Class 2, one lane dirt. Recommend a sturdy, 2-wheel or 4-wheel drive vehicle.  One steep and narrow grade, climbed successfully by a 2WD van. An enjoyable ride for bikes and motorcycles.  Vehicles should use care with soft sand near beaches. The van had to be towed out when its driver ventured too close to the water.  Interesting mountain bike and motorcycle trails.

**Supplies and Facilities:** None. You may want to gather firewood on the drive in; there is very little available at the beaches.

## TRIP LOG
### *To San Juanico Cove and Playa San Basilio*

| | |
|---|---|
| 0.0 | Turn off Transpeninsular Highway 1 at Km 49 east toward the Sea of Cortez.  Smooth dirt road, Class 1. |
| 1.0 | Ranch road to right. |
| 1.5 | Shade tree with interesting graffiti! |
| 2.1 | Fork. Go right. |
| 2.8 | Spectacular winding pass through rock spires. |
| 3.1 | Ranch. |
| 5.0 | Fork. Road divides and comes back together.  Take either fork. |
| 5.9 | Magnificent Wild Fig growing up the side of the canyon wall on right. |
| 7.0 | Junction. Turnoff right to Playa San Basilio.  Continue straight to San Juanico fish camp. |

### *To San Juanico  Fish Camp:*

| | |
|---|---|
| 7.0 | Go straight. |
| 8.9 | Palm trees on right, white rock shelves on left. |
| 9.3 | Fork. Left to *pangas* on beach. Right to San Juanico fish camp. |
| 10.2 | Beach at San Juanico. |

### To Playa San Basilio  (In San Juanico Cove)

7.0    Turn right at the 7 mile junction.

7.4    Deep, sandy wash.

8.2    Steep, narrow upgrade. A 2-wheel drive vehicle can make it.

9.5    First sighting of the sea.

9.6    Steep downgrade.

10.4    Fork. Straight leads to two beach areas. Turn right to Playa San Basilio.

10.9    You have arrived at the water's edge. Be careful of soft sand.

## Trip 14 MAP San Juanico Cove and Playa San Basilio

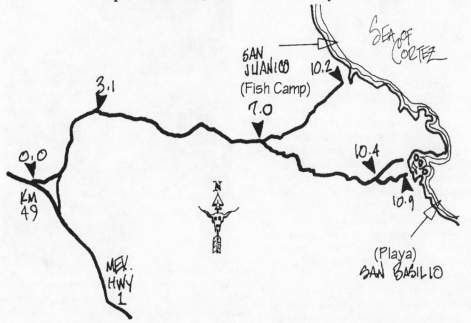

# SECTION 5 —INTRODUCTION

## CROSSING MOUNTAINS FROM SEA TO SHINING SEA

*"A 12-foot Saguaro Cactus can live on 1/50 of a quart of water a day. A date palm requires 25,000 times as much."*
Joseph Wood Krutch
*The Forgotten Peninsula*

This statement refutes the idea many people have that Baja California is nothing but dry desert. You only have to drive the back-roads of this section to realize how much water exists on the peninsula. The mountainous area between Loreto on the Sea of Cortez and the Magdalena Desert on the Pacific rises to catch the rainfall and ship the run-off through luxuriant canyons, one of which supports the Comondús, the twin villages, San José and San Miguel, established by the Padres. The run-off through the arroyos of the backcountry supports pockets of waving palms tucked away where water seeps or sometimes flows.

Replaying childhood, we stop where a wash crosses the road and wade up a stream of smooth river rock. Some pools along the way even support schools of small fish. Vines cascade down steep, multi-hued cliffs, dark with the dampness of seepage. Oh yes, the mountains of the peninsula have water: cascades, creeks, pools, ponds, and rushing

waterfalls. Stop. Turn off. Explore. Water, water, everywhere!

These trips are also about the backcountry people, settlers content to avoid our fast lane of society. The ranch people along these roads may have little spendable cash, maybe only enough from the sale of goats and cheese to buy the flour and beans they need. Yet they are not poor. They have meaningful work: caring for their herds, making cheese and leather, saddles and shoes. They have shelter without a

probably would not have even noticed her slight imperfection. Did the beautiful models on TV cause this girl's dissatisfaction with herself? Will she become anorexic and demand Calvin Klein jeans? Will the encroachment of the city violence, if seen daily, destroy the peaceful existence of these people the way it has the peace of our cities in just a few decades?

Some of our favorite adventures in the backcountry are simple by modern day standards: being shown through a ranch wife's modest garden, eating an orange off the tree of Don Alberto, feeling the softness of Francisco's tanned leather as he prepares to make a new pair of shoes. We drink water cooled in a hand-chiseled stone urn, a wedding gift from brother to brother, and climb a waterfall in so-called arid Baja California. Simple adventures, simple pleasures.

mortgage payment, and food from their animals and gardens. The closeness of family and the visits of friends and relatives provide many opportunities for fiestas.

As a few satellite dishes rise on their horizon, bringing them the non-stop marketing taking place in the "civilized" world, one can only wonder if their desires to have more will destroy their contentment. Recently we were visiting ranch friends when the young wife of one of the sons shyly produced a hair removal kit, asking Susie and me for instructions. She was unhappy with some hairs on her chin. So in a remote ranch house in the mountains, with the whole family watching, we performed a beautification treatment on a girl who a few years ago

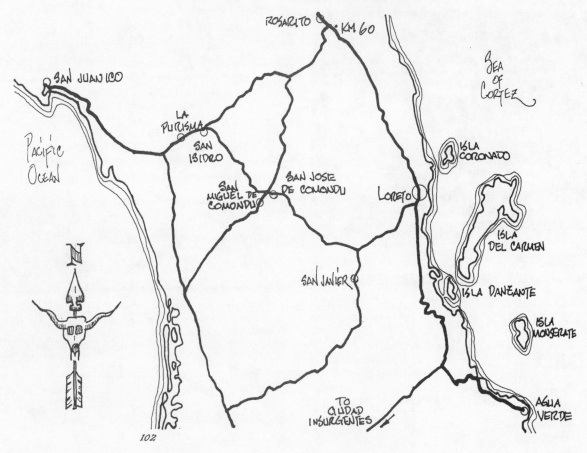

# TRIP 15

## San Juanico (on the Pacific) Through La Purísima, San Isidro to Highway 1 at Rosarito
### (Between Mulege and Loreto)

If we're just wanting to get from one side of the peninsula to the other in the mid-section, we use the graded gravel road between San Juanico, a lovely beach site on the Pacific, and Transpeninsular Highway 1, especially when the grader has recently been through and you can "fly" at 30 or 40 mph. Years ago, before this government improvement, the trip was more adventurous since it wound through the canyon floor for most of the way. The lovely scenery is still there but now we sometimes have to slow ourselves down or we miss it. Stop and walk into the arroyos. Pause to watch fish swimming in a small lake.

The lovely stone aqueduct that delivers water to La Purísima and San Isidro, the two mountain villages, makes possible the tangle of orchards and gardens crowding the roadside with colorful bloom and the fragrance of both flowers and fruit. Sadly, a shrinking population is evident in the deserted houses left vacant by the young families who must move to the more populated areas to find employment.

Sometimes we take this road in reverse with San Juanico's pristine beaches the goal. Here you can camp along the sand if you have a 4-wheel drive and are careful about how you use it. The beach around the bay is wide and smooth, perfect for tent camping, swimming and surf fishing.

Scorpion Bay, world famous for multiple sets of surf, turns a surfer into an Ever Ready, who just keeps going and going and going. We've never been there in the summer months when this heavy surf occurs but the tanned young men of the sport tell us the rides are so long they take turns driving each other from a terminal pick-up spot back out to the first break so they can catch another ride without the long swim.

The Scorpion Bay Campground is located on the bluffs over this action area. Campsites are literally on the edge, looking down at a dramatic rocky shoreline. The open-air palapa restaurant-bar is pleasant, also with an ocean view.

An ideal circle trip with some adventure travel mixed in is to leave Mulege and cross over to the Pacific via La Ballena, (see Trip 9) or S. J. de Las Pilas (see Trip 10) to San Juanico, then return on this faster road.

**Length of Trip:** 71.6 miles.
**Road Condition:** Class 1. Frequent grading keeps this road in fair condition. Some washboarding. Because of the sharp, fist-sized-rock surface, it is a bumpy ride for bikes and cycles.
**Fuel:** San Juanico, San Isidro.
**Supplies:** Staples in San Juanico, La Purísima, San Isidro. Small restaurants in San Juanico, sometimes open.
**Lodging:** Hotel: None.
**Campground**: San Juanico, on Scorpion Bay. Hot showers, restaurant.

## TRIP LOG

0.0    Leave San Juanico toward La Purísima through typical coastal desert of sparse vegetation.

19.8    Turn-off to San Gregorio, a small fishing community with good surfing. Use care through the one lane Arroyo Los Burros where the road usually is very badly washboarded.

26.9    Climb the "La Purísima grade" then drop downhill to palms and a water-filled arroyo.

28.9    Turn left to La Purísima and PAVEMENT! Insurgentes is to the right.

32.6    Turn-off into the villages of El Zapote and El Cheflon.

33.5    Village of La Purísima. On left, Restaurant Claudia and a store that has ICE!

36.0    Picturesque village of San Isidro. Here you can usually buy gasoline from barrels, even Magna Sin, although it's wise to fill up before leaving on this trip.

36.6    Pavement ends at the sign, "S J de Comondú 30, Rosarito 58." This section of road shows off the village with the old stone aqueduct running down one side and the orchards and gardens dense with fruit and blooms on the other. The narrow road through the village usually requires some pulling over or backing up to make room for another vehicle to pass.

37.5    Road turns left, then a road goes left to Paso Hondo. Continue straight.

| | | | |
|---|---|---|---|
| 38.1 | A small store, *Tienda Rural*, on right. The graded road leaving town has minimal washboarding. | 56.1 | Km 29 The road is rocky-rough through this section, rather than washboard, with several picturesque small ranchos. |
| 39.0 | SIGN! Rosarito, left. Comondú, straight. Turn left and begin climb out of La Purísima- San Isidro area. | 58.4 | A series of narrow, sharp curves. Watch for opposing traffic. |
| 40.1 | Stop for magnificent vista of the valley and towns with the distinctive El Pilar mountain towering over all. | 60.4 | The "adventurous" road to the Comondús on right (SEE TRIP 16). Continue straight toward Rosarito. |
| 45.0 | Road on left to Ejido Los Naranjos. | 61.6 | Road on left to El Crucerito Ranch. Several roads cut off right. Stay on graded road, straight. |
| 46.3 | Ranch on left and a lake that in normal years boasts a population of small fish. This is a nice picnic stop. The road drops down to the valley floor then up the other side through stands of mature Cardón and, in spring, the brilliant yellow of Palo Verde bloom. | 71.6 | Transpeninsular Highway 1 at Km 60, Rosarito. |

## TRIP 15 MAP

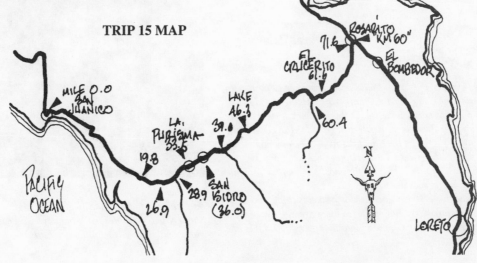

# TRIP 16
## Old Road Comondú
### (From Transpeninsular Hwy 1 at Rosarito to the Comondús, San Isidro & return to Hwy 1).

*"...most drivers will find that the known trails of Baja are going to offer them about all the excitement, danger and reward they will be able to stomach in one lifetime."*

Jim Hunter
*Off-beat Baja*

For 4x4 thrills, the 25-plus mile stretch between El Crucerito and San José de Comondú must compare with driving the downed freeways after the L. A. earthquake. Since this segment of road is only used by a few ranchers these days, mostly at each end to travel out to the main roads, but NOT to cross over the hills from the Comondús to El Crucerito on the road between La Purisima and the highway; this horrendous jumble, besides crossing the most stupendous rockpile imaginable, is no longer maintained.

Anyone with any sense, and respect for their vehicle and tires, would go the San Isidro way. But of course there are those who see a line on the map as a challenge. Shortly into the trip I dubbed this one "Rocky Trails."

As with many Baja trails, choosing the bad over the good takes you up, in this case on a very bad climb, over broken slabs, often tilted with sharp edges, through boulders, over boulders, shale, and loose stuff that isn't too stable on inclines. To travel a road through this is to wonder, who moved the thousands of boulders along the road side to

make vehicle passage possible? And why? Like the chicken, I guess, to get to the other side?

The entire 87.9 mile loop is goat country, and little wonder. Lava slides of caramel-colored stones, some piled, some laid out like pavers, cover the landscape for miles in every direction.

Yet there, smack in the middle of Flintstone heaven, the Padres decided to build a mission. So suddenly, you start downhill and are taken back by the sight of a true oasis of thick green palms, San José de Comondú, one of the twin towns that have managed to remain Shangri-las in the desert. Abundant water is obvious as the villages bloom with lush gardens and orchards.

*After creeping over miles of rock and more rock, the quiet setting of the restored mission explains the Padre's choice of site.*

*The less-adventurous, or those without a sturdy, 4-wheel drive vehicle, can skip the loop section of this trip and visit the Comondús by way of the San Isidro road or by using Trip 17 or 18..*

**Trip Length:** 87.9 miles.

**Road Condition:** Class 1 from Rosarito to El Crucerito turn-off. Class 3 for the middle portion of the 25 miles to the Comondús from the El Crucerito turn-off. Class 1 and 2 on the Comondú to San Isidro stretch. Class 1 on the San Isidro-El Crucerito portion. Four-wheel drive recommended on the El Crucerito-San Jose de Comondú segment. A challenging dirt bike ride. *Very* difficult for mountain bikes.

**Supplies and Facilities:**
> **Fuel:** San Isidro, yes. Comondús, sometimes in barrels but don't count on it.
> **Food:** Small markets for staples in the Comondús and San Isidro.
> **Hotel or Campground:** No.

# TRIP LOG
*Rosarito/Comondús Loop Trip*

0.0   Turn off Transpeninsular Highway 1 at Km 60. The highway is signed coming from both north and south, "San Isidro." The signs on the road after the turn-off show the kilometer distance to San Isidro, 61 and La Purisima, 65.

This trip begins on a straight, graded gravel Class 1 road which can be smooth if the grader has been by recently or washboarded if not.

4.0   Cemented *vados* (dips). Slow down as they often have a sharp edge between dirt and pavement that can do serious damage to tires.

7.0   Upgrade and curves but wide enough for two vehicles to pass.

10.0   El Crucerito Ranch (signed), on right.

11.3   Take turn-off, left.

12.7   Cattle guard and fence. The road is well-traveled so far. It crosses a wash then enters a forest of trees. Watch the height if driving a high clearance camper.

13.8   Fork. Continue straight.

15.6   Fork. Turn right toward the hills.

16.2   Fork. Go right. Begin a very bad climb over shale, sharp slabs, washed out boulders.

16.9   Fork. Go straight. If you have time to look, there's a great view of the green valley you've just left.

17.0   Road smooths out as you approach a wooden cattle guard and fence.

18.0   Old ranch and corral on left. Continue to drive slide area of rock, dotted with Cardón and Pitahaya. Very loose rock road bed.

19.4   Continue straight past roads entering from left and right. Begin another very loose, very narrow climb. Use low gears and creep. My notes say, "Not for the faint-hearted."

| | |
|---|---|
| 20.1 | ANOTHER rough climb over flat slabs interspersed with loose rock, all edged by boulders. This is goat country! |
| 21.4 | Short reprieve of smoother road. |
| 21.7 | Begin downgrade. |
| 23.2 | Small ranch on right. Road flattens out and improves, then worsens, crossing boulder field. |
| 24.5 | Ranch on right. Goat, of course. Road climbs once more, easier, more highly-traveled. Smooths enough for 20 to 25 mph, but not for long. The road matches the rockpiles alongside. |
| 29.2 | Fork. Stay right. Pass two ranches. |
| 33.6 | Downgrade past pile-upon-pile of carmel-colored rock. |
| 35.5 | Look down and left to the palms of San Jose de Comondú! |
| 35.9 | Junction. Right to San Isidro. Left to Comondús. Turn left. |
| 36.7 | Road deadends at main street of San Jose de Comondú. Road left to San Javier. Road right to Poso Grande. (After sight-seeing, return to this crossroad and backtrack). |
| 37.5 | When you reach this junction, turn left toward San Isidro. |
| 37.6 | Cemetery on right. The road is Class 2, the surrounding terrain still all rock. |
| 43.0 | Hill with microwave tower on left, ranch on right. |
| 51.8 | Vista of the valley with road climbing far mountains to Paso Hondo. The dramatic El Pilar monument-shaped mountain is on the left. |
| 55.3 | Turn right back toward Transpeninsular Hwy 1, straight ahead goes to San Isidro and La Purisima. |

| | |
|---|---|
| 62.3 | Road to left, signed, to Ejido Los Naranjos |
| 62.6 | Lake on right. With normal rainfall the lake is home to small fish. Scenic drive over Class 1 road. |
| 74.7 | Narrow, sharp curves. Watch for opposing traffic. |
| 76.2 | Concrete dips (*vados*), with sharp edges, reduce speed. |
| 77.9 | El Crucerito Ranch, again. |
| 87.9 | Transpeninsular Highway 1. Driving our '74, 4WD Chevy pick-up with an 8-foot camper, and taking time for lunch but no sightseeing in the villages, the loop trip took us 5 1/2 hours. |

## Tips for Rough Trips

Take it slow. The nearest repair shop is many boulders away.

Carry plenty of water, food and spare parts.

Keep your meals, especially dinners, quick and easy. A can of beans and weinies tastes like fillet mignon when you're dusty, hungry and ready for your sleeping bag.

# TRIP 16 MAP Old Road Comondú Loop

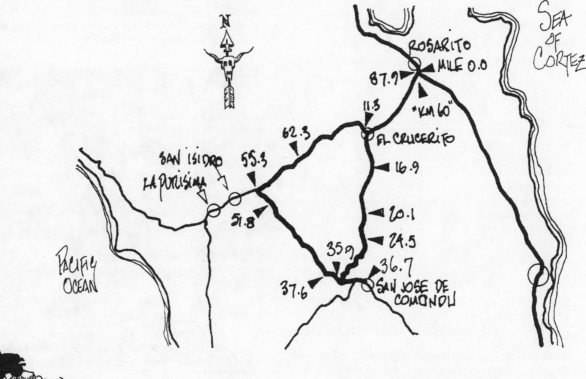

N

SEA OF CORTEZ

ROSARITO
MILE 0.0
87.9
11.3
"KM 60"
62.3
EL CRUCERITO
SAN ISIDRO
LA PURISIMA
55.3
16.9
51.8
20.1
24.5
35.9
36.7
37.6
SAN JOSE DE COMONDU

PACIFIC OCEAN

109

# TRIP 17

## The Comondús from the (Back and Beautiful) Side
(State Highway 53 to the two Comondú villages, San Miguel  and San José to Loreto)

Climbing off the sparsely-vegetated Magdalena Desert through canyons of palms, thick vegetation and trees, fresh running streams and tumbles of exotic rock formations, awakens the senses like many of the peninsula's backroads. The road coming from the Pacific side of the peninsula to the twin villages, San José' de Comondú and San Miguel de Comondú, ranks high in Baja beauty. It's sometimes necessary to stop and allow the eyes a rest as one scene of magnificence after another bombards our over-stimulated senses.

The settlement of Comondú was begun in 1708 with a chapel and a few huts for the converted Indians. Later the mission at San José was begun. It is reported the Padres had 160,000 mule-loads of soil brought in to plant fruit trees and grapes. The luxuriant vegetation and gardens lining the road between the villages seems to confirm the truth of this statement. The entire settlement exudes cheer. Colonial-style buildings of red brick sit in the midst of flower-filled yards and residents wave a friendly greeting as you pass by.

The slow, quiet life of the towns is nowhere more evident than the site of the small mission in San José. A few small children run in the small plaza as their mothers chat on the steps of the small market. The mission sits in a hush, its bell silent and as we walk inside, even our footsteps on the old stone seem muffled by the cushion of time.

No lovelier drive can be possible than through the Eden that exists between the villages. On one side of the narrow road high bluffs blackened with varnish, provide shade. Opposite, a lovely rock wall

attempts to contain semi-tended gardens of overgrown plants living in luxuriant harmony. The feeling of happiness and well-being is so prevalent throughout this area, you can actually feel it caressing the skin like a warm breeze.

**Trip Length:** 51.9 miles.

**Road Condition:** Class 1 and 2. Some straight hard-packed sand stretches with rough mountain climbs and arroyos mixed in. A challenge for mountain bikers. Fun for dirt bikes.

**Supplies and Facilities:**
>  **Fuel:** Sometimes in barrels in the villages, but don't count on it.
>  **Supplies:** Small market across the plaza from the mission in San José de Comondú.
>  **Lodging:** No

# TRIP LOG

*State Hwy 53 to the two Comondú villages to Loreto.*

0.0    Turn off paved State Highway 53 at Km 64 (signed), "Comondús 31 km." This is a graded gravel, high-speed road, passing flat, dry, low desert vegetation.

12.0    Ranchos Los Pajaros (The birds) on right. The scenery improves as the hills increase.

14.5    Rancho Medio Corral. The road passes through a canyon tumbling with giant blocks of rock.

16.1    Adobe ruin on right. Palms spread through the canyon indicating a water source.

16.7    Small cemetery on left.

17.0    Rancho El Ranchito.

18.4    Canyon narrows at Rancho Piedra Rodada. Road narrows as it continues through this lovely canyon of sheer cliffs, caves, palms and trees.

21.0    Rancho Pte. De Madera. Wide one-lane road climbs to a perfect look-out/photo stopping spot.

21.9    Two tiled shrines on the rock wall look down into another arroyo of gardens and orchards.

22.9    Sign for San Miguel de Comondú.

23.1    Turn right and continue straight to the other twin, San José de Comondú. The two are linked by a narrow tropical road. Go to dead-end and turn left. Follow brick wall on left.

24.6    Enter San José de Comondú.

25.0    Sign for San Javier, straight. Turn left toward San Isidro/La Purisima.

25.1    Market on right and the small plaza. The mission is across the plaza. Ask at the market for person with the key to unlock the building. A small donation will be appreciated.

25.4    Sign: "Las Parras." Continue straight on narrow, one-lane road. This portion of the road is very narrow for motorhomes.

25.9    Sign: "Loreto 78
>>>>>> Las Parras 48
>>>>>> San Javier 42".

Continue straight as road climbs up mountain. This is a one-lane graded road around the mountain. Drive slowly and watch for on-coming traffic.

26.6    Sign: San Javier 36 Km. The road is straight, one lane graded with some dips and rough spots that quickly deteriorates. Narrow, rough with areas of loose gravel.

## Backroad Enchiladas

8 corn tortillas
One 8 oz. can enchilada sauce
One onion, chopped
One 4 oz. can whole kernel corn, drained
Two zucchini, chopped
One green pepper, chopped
1/2 cup of jack, cheddar or goat cheese, grated

Heat enchilada sauce in small saucepan. Saute vegetables until hot but still crunchy. Heat tortillas to soften. Fill each tortilla with vegetables: Roll up, seam side down, two to a plate. Pour sauce over and sprinkle with cheese. Cover with foil for a few minutes to melt cheese.

| | |
|---|---|
| 30.0 | Old ranch, left. Probably an outpost camp used only intermittently. Rough road with more ranches continues. |
| 31.6 | San Telmo Ranch followed by a rough stretch of road. |
| 35.9 | Old stone oven on left. Cross a wash. This is the route of the "Baja 1000" road race. |
| 38.1 | Road climbs with sharp switchbacks. Definitely not a motorhome road. Use care and low gear. |
| 39.0 | Sign: "Puerta Vieja Km 21". Slight upgrade to ranch at top. |
| 40.0 | Nice lunch stop on left, overlooking deep arroyo. |
| 42.1 | Rancho Chino. Road smooths out as it continues through ranch country. |

| | |
|---|---|
| 47.3 | After Rancho San Guillermo on right, the road narrows and follows the arroyo through gradual grades. |
| 50.9 | Junction. Signed: Las Parras 17, arrow for San Javier, right. A right turn is backtracking. With a high-clearance vehicle, turn left onto a shortcut. This is a rough and rocky trail that fords a stream. |
| 51.9 | Ranch. Road passes around buildings and meets the road to San Javier. Bear left to Loreto. |

### Patti's Tip of the Day

Fresh corn tortillas are a quick meal staple for camping trips but they will mold very quickly. Unwrap and spread them out on a towel to cool and dry. Turn once, then after a few minutes rewrap in paper, not plastic.

# TRIP 17 MAP The Comondús from the Back (and Beautiful) Side

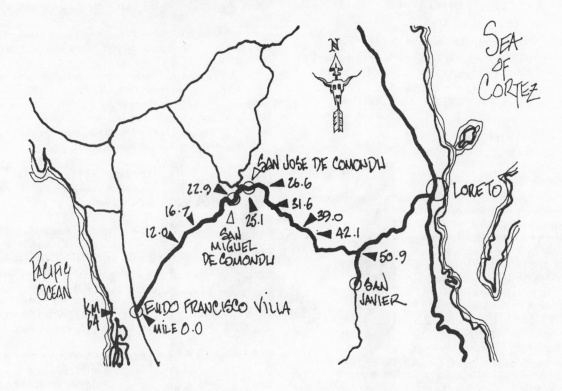

N

SEA OF CORTEZ

SAN JOSE DE COMONDU

22.9    26.6

16.7    31.6

12.0    25.1    39.0

SAN MIGUEL DE COMONDU    42.1

50.9

LORETO

PACIFIC OCEAN

SAN JAVIER

KM 64

EJIDO FRANCISCO VILLA

MILE 0.0

# TRIP 18

## Misión San Javier and Beyond

(One mile south of Loreto to San Javier and State Hwy 53 at 2.3 miles north of Colonia Purisima, on Pacific side of the peninsula).

*"All good roads are alike; every bad road is bad in its own way."*

Joseph Wood Krutch
*The Forgotten Peninsula*

The circular stone stairway leading up to the bell tower of the ancient mission is no longer accessible for visitors to the lovely, restored moorish building but the sanctuary tour is still open to the public. Re-enacting the trip made by Padre Francisco Píccolo through the rugged Sierra Gigantas to the location of Misión San Javier emphasizes why it took the Jesuit and his flock more than a decade to complete this lovely stone church. The second of the Baja California missions was not finished until 1758, six years after the completion of Mission Nuestra Senora de Loreto, the oldest mission of the Californias.

When you stop at the mission, a caretaker will appear to unlock the building and escort you around. On December 2, this

sleepy town awakens up with a two day fiesta to celebrate San Javier day.

The drive is lovely and continues so, although the road deteriorates past San Javier, becoming more adventurous as it crosses to the other side of the peninsula.

*It's a perfect "take-your-time" kind of road that forces you to relax and enjoy your surroundings. We stopped to talk to a rancher at one point. I had my door open to catch the breeze and felt something tickling my arm. The whiskers of a curious burro!*

Blacktopped Hwy 53 will take you to Ciudad Insurgentes to the south or La Purisima and San Juanico, north.

**Trip Length:** 22.1 miles to Misión San Javier, 65.8 miles from Transpeninsular Highway 1 to State Highway 53, paved.

**Road Condition:** Begins Class 1, then Class 2 to San Javier. Autos and tour vans from Loreto drive it. Road deteriorates to Class 3 in places after San Javier. Dual-purpose motorcyclers and mountain bikers will find this an enjoyable ride to the mission. Beyond, the road is a 4x4 and dirt bike challenge due to areas of large river rock.

**Supplies & Facilities:**
    **Fuel:** Loreto.
    **Supplies:** Small store in San Javier.
                Restaurant La Palapa.
    **Lodging:** None.

# TRIP LOG

0.0    Signed turn-off 1.1 miles south of Loreto. Sign reads (in kilometers) to: Comondu 71, San Javier 36, Las Parras 20. Road is graded gravel, heading toward the diorama of one hill superimposed on the next, reaching to the rugged peaks of the Sierra Gigantas. Some washboard, rolling knolls and slight grades, all limiting the speed to between 20 and 40, depending upon when the grader last passed through.

6.4    Corral at bottom of wash. Road climbs again through narrow rock walls.

7.3    Small shrine on right.

9.3    One lane around ridge of mountain. Watch for opposing traffic.

10.2    Excellent photo spot and wide enough to pull over and stop. You can see the sea behind and look down into the deep canyon.

10.7    El Pilon de Parras, the sheer peak you've been seeing for some time, narrows the road on the right. Use slow speed in this area.

11.9    Rancho Las Parras. This ranch boasts a small stone church and orchards. In season, you can buy fresh oranges. The road continues to climb. If you've left in the morning the sun is pleasantly at your back.

13.0    The land flattens out onto a wide plain. The road widens to two lane.

14.9    Brick ranch house on left, then continue through a lush canyon bottom, thick with trees and cacti.

16.3    Wash, running with water except in drought years. Rancho Viejo on right. On our visit, a flock of turkeys were drinking at the spring.

17.8    Turn-off on right to the Comondús. (See Trip 16). Watch for opposing traffic all along this road since it is the main route for San Javier residents.

20.9    Watch for loose rocks on road.

21.9    The village of San Javier. Bear right at stop sign into town.

22.1    Misión San Javier. To continue, when facing the mission bear left and then right past a small picturesque brick house. The road immediately becomes one lane, rocky, cobbled.

22.6    Road continues to deteriorate. At this point, we locked in our hubs.

23.2    El Segundo Paso, a ranch of neat garlic fields, arbors and palms, on right.

23.6    Rancho Segundo Paso. After passing a rough cobbled wash, the road widens and smooths out while passing through beds of river rock and passes rich with mature Old Man cacti, Mesquite, quail, dove and ground squirrels darting over spills of lava rock.

25.1    Sign: La Fortuna, left, Palo Blanco, straight. Continue straight.

25.3    Continue straight at the Las Juntas fork.

26.8    La Presa Vieja (The old dam) Ranch on right. Road is sandy now. Enjoy the moment since it changes quickly to rough cobble.

27.6    Very neat red brick ranch on left.

29.3    Rancho Agua Escondida. Road smooths out over hard sand.

30.2    The very neat ranch, Poza de Gonzalez.

31.1    BAD boulder area! Need high clearance vehicle to creep over high, sharp rock, followed by more rough cobble.

| | |
|---|---|
| 31.6 | Fork. Stay right. Km 16 sign, El Peloteado. |
| 31.9 | Picturesque and prosperous Rancho Santo Domingo, on right. Cultivated fields and orchard nestled beneath steep, varnish-stained cliffs. The road continues to alternate between rough cobble and smooth sand. |
| 34.1 | Fork, bear left. Very rough boulder and cobble wash. |
| 35.1 | Fork, bear right. |
| 38.8 | Rancho El Eden. |
| 40.7 | Rancho Palo Blanco. |
| 44.5 | Ranch, on right. |
| 45.0 | Ranch, right. Numerous forks branch off to detours used during wet weather. All rejoin but use most recently traveled. |
| 50.8 | Good sand road and open areas. Notice the ball moss, a plant dependent on moisture from the air. The flat terrain and sparse vegetation signals the closer proximity to the Pacific. |
| 55.0 | Rancho Piedra Parada. The road allows a little more speed now. |
| 60.6 | Closed gate. The civilization of cultivated farm land and power lines. |
| 65.8 | Paved Highway 53. |

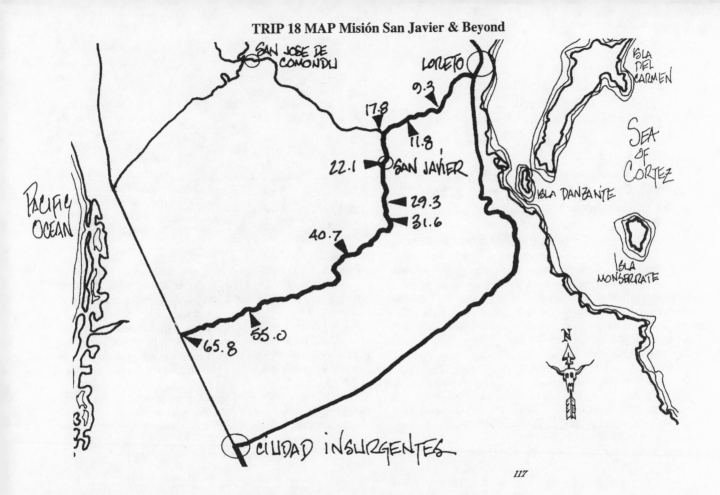

SAN JOSE DE COMONDU

LORETO

9.3

17.8

11.8

22.1

SAN JAVIER

29.3

31.6

40.7

55.0

65.8

PACIFIC OCEAN

CIUDAD INSURGENTES

ISLA DEL CARMEN

SEA OF CORTEZ

ISLA DANZANTE

ISLA MONSERRATE

N

30
35

# TRIP 19
## Agua Verde
(Turn-off at Km 64, south of Loreto, to Agua Verde and the Sea of Cortez)

*"The stone mountains pile up to the sky and there is little fresh water. But we know we must go back if we live, and we don't know why."*
John Steinbeck
*The Log from The Sea of Cortez*

*The bay of Agua Verde, not many years ago, was the private domain of the few fishermen and their families who lived in virtual isolation in a small village along the Sea of Cortez. Their families tended the goats, walked beaches and probably stared out at the distant islands wondering what other life existed. The first time we arrived with a gathering of friends, I'm certain many of those question marks disappeared. We brought sailboards, an Avon for diving, a 18-foot aluminum boat for fishing and waterskiing, and a baby goat one of our trucks almost ran down on the highway. She was so tiny and alone, Ed put her in the front of the pickup at Carol's feet and off she went to find a stepmother. Within the day little "Camina" (named after her highway adoption) had found a new home and a mother willing to feed her. The residents of Agua Verde thought we were very interesting. The young men dressed up in their best western hats and boots and came to the* beach to observe us at play in the water or to our camp where they sat on their haunches for hours satisfied to watch us cook and listen to our strange language. Even the children would rarely accept our hospitality of food or even candy. The people of Agua Verde are shy yet friendly and seemed content with a welcome break in the monotony of their isolated life.

Since this all-weather harbor has long been a favorite with boats traveling north and south on the Sea of Cortez, the people did get used to *gringos*. The lovely setting was so popular with the sailboaters, they even erected a small yacht club on shore. Then the government decided to build a graded gravel road to get the fishermen's catch to market more efficiently. We visited Agua Verde about five years ago, for the first time for us by road, not knowing what changes easier access had made. Except for a few campers along the shore, we saw little difference from the times we had visited by boat.

As you travel toward Agua Verde from the highway over the mountains above the beaches, many roads down to the shore are visible. Short of camping in someone's front yard, you are welcome to choose any spot along the shore.

The bay is sheltered and ideal for kayaking and swimming. An afternoon breeze is usually available for board sailing or just to cool things down.

We were afraid on our last visit that the village might have grown into another Cabo or a "gringoland." But not so. The goats still visit your campsite if you camp near the village. Like many ranches in the backcountry, the evenings at Agua Verde quiet down quite early as most of the residents go to bed at dark.

Agua Verde is a lovely place to camp, fish, snorkel, dive, sail and swim — or just sit and gaze out at the Sea of Cortez.

**Length of Trip:** 50 miles, roundtrip.

**Road condition:** Class 1. Suitable for 2-wheel drive. Adventurous drivers of small motorhomes do travel this road, although much of it is up and down grades with several tight switchbacks. We make no recommendations for this type of vehicle although we did tow an 18-foot aluminum boat to the beach here several years ago without incident. The road surface depends on the last visit by the grader. Some tough grades for mountain bikers but the views are worth the effort. Great trip for dual-purpose motorcycles.

**Supplies & Facilities:**

**Fuel:** No.

**Supplies:** Small market for staples. Two small restaurants for simple fare.

**Lodging:** None.

Bring your own firewood. It is scarce, and the villagers need what is available.

# TRIP LOG

*Turnoff at Km 64, south of Loreto, to Agua Verde on the Sea of Cortez.*

0.0     Turn-off, 35.7 miles south of Loreto, at Km 64 (Signed, Agua Verde, 41) 25.9 miles.

1.6     First vista of the mountains and the monument formations of the peaks. The road is graded gravel with some washboarding through pleasant dips and curves. This is a dry desert area; the beauty is in the rock formations and mountain views.

4.1     Road on right, with sign, Santa Cruz, 6.

4.3     Rancho Viejo, on right.

5.1     Ultima Agua, 1 Km, (sign) on right. Road follows wash, rough in some spots, then climbs.

10.5    This first view of the Sea of Cortez and the offshore island, Santa Catalina, is breathtaking. The road descends rapidly and twists and turns with many sharp switchbacks. There are several turnouts should you meet another vehicle, or if you choose to stop and enjoy the view.

14.1    At the bottom of the hill is a sign, "Ranchita San Cosme, Soda, Tortillas, Hot Pools", then the Restaurant San Cosme. The restaurant is small, serving simple Mexican fare. You can park anywhere and hike along the beach past the one trailer to the hot thermal pools. The walk is about one kilometer or it can be driven with a 4x4 at low tide. Here, and at all of the beaches, use care with the soft sand. Vehicles can get stuck very quickly. Although you have reached the bay, the village is at the far southern end.

18.2    *"Zona de Vados"* (Dips). Paved *vados* can do tire damage at higher speed, use care.

| 22.2 | Another climb. The road winds along the edge of the hills rather than low on the beach. The road is graded with some rough spots. |
|---|---|
| 24.5 | A government-built water tank, supplying potable water to the village. |

24.9 *"Restaurante Agua Verde"*, supplying beer, soda, tortillas, fishing guide/panga excursions. You have arrived. Turn left to the beach or continue right past the village homes, school and small market. You will find shady campsites at the beach but little privacy since there are several small homes nearby.

## TRIP 19 MAP Agua Verde

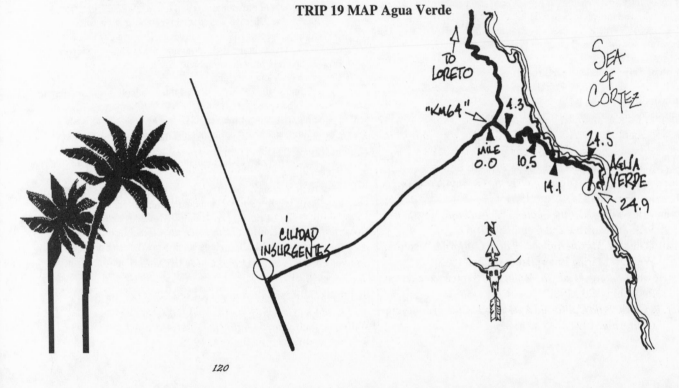

# BOOK LIST

Cannon, Ray. *The Sea of Cortez.* Menlo Park: Lane Books, 1966.

Crosby, Harry W. *Antigua California, Mission and Colony on the Peninsular Frontier, 1697-1768.* Albuquerque: University of New Mexico Press, 1994.

Crosby, Harry W. *The Cave Paintings of Baja* . Salt Lake City: Copley Books, 1984.

Crow, T. James and Murray, Spencer. *Off-Roader's Handbook.* Los Angeles: HPBooks, 1986.

Crumpton, Landon. *Baja Almanac.* San Diego, 1996.

Farley, Michael B. & L. K. *Diving Mexico's Baja California* Port Hueneme, CA: Marcor Enterprises, 1980.

Forgey, Wm, M.D. *Wilderness Medicine.* 4th Edition.

Gardner, Erle Stanley. *Hovering Over Baja.* New York:Wm. Morrow and Company, 1961.

Gardner, Erle Stanley. *Off the Beaten Track in Baja.* New York: William Morrow and Company, 1967.

Gotshall, Daniel W. *Marine Animals of Baja California.* Ventura: Western Marine Enterprises, 1982.

Hale, Howard. *Long Walk to Mulege.* Santee: Pinkerton Publishing Co., 1980.

Hunter, R. Clark. *Baja California Automobile Club of Southern California.* 1993.

Hunter, Jim. *Offbeat Baja.* San Francisco: Chronicle Books, 1977.

Johnson, William Weber. *Baja California.* Time Life Books, 1972.

Krutch, Joseph Wood. *The Forgotten Peninsula.* William Sloan Associates, 1961.

Lewellyn, Harry. *Backroad Trips and Tips.* Anaheim: Glovebox Publications, 1993.

Mackintosh, Graham. *Into A Desert Place.* Inglewood: Graham Mackintosh, 1990.

McMahan, Mike. *Adventures in Baja.* Los Angeles: Mc Mahan Bros. Desk Co.,Inc., 1983.

Merrick, Harry. *Baja Traveler.* Airguide Publications, 1988.

Minch, John & Leslie, Thomas. *The Baja Highway.* San Juan Capistrano: John Minch and Assoc. Inc., 1993.

Murray, Spencer & Poole, Ralph. *Cruising The Sea of Cortez.* Palm Desert: Best-West Publications, 1963.

Potter, Ginger. *Baja Book IV.* El Cajon: Baja Source, 1996.

Roberts, Norman C. *Baja California Plant and Field Guide.* La Jolla: Natural History Publishing Co. , 1989.

Sawyer Products. *A Practical Guide to Outdoor Protection.* 1994.

Steinbeck, John, and Edward R. Ricketts. *The Log from the Sea of Cortez.* New York: Viking Press, 1941.

Williams, Jack. *The Magnificent Peninsula.* Salt Lake City: H.J Williams Publications, 1995.

*WANT TO ORDER ADDITIONAL COPIES FOR FAMILY AND*
*FRIENDS? OR ORDER copies of our SEAFOOD COOKBOOKS?*
*Just fill out the form below and send a check or money order to:*
*Somethin's Fishy Publications*
*P. O. Box 2010*
*Sparks NV 89432*

-------------------------------------------------------------

Please send:

\_\_copy(s)Backroad Baja (124 pages)   $15.95 _____

        Outside U.S.  17.95 _____

\_\_copy(s)Somethin's Fishy in Baja (200 pages) 14.95 _____

        Outside U.S.  16.95 _____

\_\_copy(s)Seafood Baja-Style (20 postcard book) 7.95 _____

       Outside U.S.  8.95 _____

     plus postage & handling per copy 3.50 _____

            *TOTAL* _____

*NAME* _____

*STREET* _____

*CITY,STATE,ZIP*_____

*COUNTRY* _____

By credit card, mail to: **Discover Baja, 3065 Clairemont Dr., San Diego, CA 92117.**

    Please charge my **MasterCard  Visa**

    Account Number _____

    Expiration Date _____

    Signature _____

# INDEX

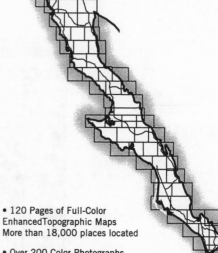